Claude-Hélène Mayer, Christian Martin Boness

Intercultural Mediation & Conflict Resolution

Cover Design:
Graphic by © Dietmar Coesebrink, Göttingen, Germany 1996

The original version of this book was published by Waxmann Verlag, Münster, in 2004 with the title
Claude-Hélène Mayer, Christian Martin Boness (2004):
„Interkulturelle Mediation und Konfliktbearbeitung. Bausteine deutsch-afrikanischer Wirklichkeiten."
© *2004 Waxmann Verlag GmbH Münster, www.waxmann.com*

Translated and Revised Version 2005
Translated by Dr Robert R. Barr, USA
Authors' Contact:
Institut für Interkulturelle Praxis & Konfliktmanagement (IIPK), Göttingen, Germany
info@interkulturelle-mediation.de, www.interkulturelle-mediation.de

Claude Hélène Mayer und Christian Martin Boness

INTERCULTURAL MEDIATION & CONFLICT RESOLUTION

ibidem-Verlag
Stuttgart

Bibliografische Information Der Deutschen Bibliothek

Die Deutsche Bibliothek verzeichnet diese Publikation in der Deutschen Nationalbibliografie; detaillierte bibliografische Daten sind im Internet über <http://dnb.ddb.de> abrufbar.

∞
Gedruckt auf alterungsbeständigem, säurefreien Papier
Printed on acid-free paper

ISBN: 3-89821-531-8

© *ibidem*-Verlag
Stuttgart 2005
Alle Rechte vorbehalten

Das Werk einschließlich aller seiner Teile ist urheberrechtlich geschützt. Jede Verwertung außerhalb der engen Grenzen des Urheberrechtsgesetzes ist ohne Zustimmung des Verlages unzulässig und strafbar. Dies gilt insbesondere für Vervielfältigungen, Übersetzungen, Mikroverfilmungen und elektronische Speicherformen sowie die Einspeicherung und Verarbeitung in elektronischen Systemen.

Printed in Germany

To
Blanche-Philhippa

Table of Contents

Foreword	9
1. Introduction	13
2. Introduction to the Assemblage of Conceptual Subjects	19
2.1 Culture, Inter-Culturality, and Values	19
2.2 The Meaning and Importance of Conflict	25
2.3 Conflicts in Intercultural Contexts—A Question of Realities?	29
3. Introduction to Mediation in the Western Context	35
3.1 What is Mediation?	35
3.2 Areas of the Application of Mediation	39
3.3 What Is the Course of the Mediation Process?	40
3.4 Techniques of Mediation	44
3.5 Non-Violent-Communication (NVC) according to Marshall Rosenberg	49
3.6 The Role of the Mediator	52
4 Introduction to Mediation	55
4.1 Application to a Third Person	55
4.2 What Is Intercultural Mediation?	56
4.3 Areas of Approach in Intercultural Mediation	61
4.4. Dealing with Western Techniques in Intercultural Mediation	62
4.5 The Role of the Mediator in Intercultural Mediation	65
4.6 Challenges in Situations of Intercultural Mediation	67
4.6.1 Styles of Conflict	67
4.6.2 Mechanisms of Conflict-Resolution and Models of Conflict-Solving	72
4.6.3 Culturalization	73
4.6.4 Prejudices and Stereotypes	74
4.6.5 Culture as a Strategy	77
4.6.6 Emotions	77
4.6.7 Power and Power Imbalances	80

4.6.8	Dynamics of Escalation in Situations of Intercultural Conflict	88
4.7	Cultural Orientation and its Consequences	91
4.8	Intercultural Influences on the Setting of Mediation	104
5.	Mediating Interaction between Westeners and Africans	111
5.1	Introduction to Cultural Dimensions of Southern Africa	111
5.2	Conflictive Constellations in Western-African Interactions	114
5.3	African Conflict-Management in the Context of Southern Africa	121
5.4	Typical Conflict Situations between Westeners and Africans	124
5.5	African Cultural Paradigms and their Effects on Western-African Mediation Processes	130
5.6.	Possibilities for Mediation in Western-African Situations of Conflict	150
5.6.1	Examples of African Mediation in Intercultural Contexts	150
5.6.2	Foundations of Western-African Mediation Settings	155
6.	Training Opportunities for the Acquisition of Mediation-Related Inter-Cultural Competency	169
6.1	Acquisition of Intercultural Competency	169
6.2	The Development of an Intercultural Personality	171
6.3	Methods of Acquisition of Intercultural Competency	175
6.4	Cultural Self-Experiencing and Cultural Alienation	178
6.5	Case Studies	180
6.6	Cultural Assimilators	182
6.7	Exercises in Alienation	188
6.8	Simulations and Role-Playing	194
6.9	A Western-African Mediation Simulation	195
7.	Outlook	203
8.	Bibliography	205

Foreword

The book at hand--Intercultural Mediation and Conflict Resolution--develops theoretical and practical questions on the subject of mediation in intercultural contexts. On a theoretical level, it undertakes explanations of concepts apropos of culture, conflict, and interculturality. Then aspects of content are explained, that of mediation, and especially, that of intercultural mediation. Concretely, these matters will be elucidated in terms of the example of Western-African interaction or situations of mediation.

The purpose of this book is an approach the complex subject of intercultural mediation, through concrete, "culturally specific" examples. These examples will be developed with the help of an analysis of cultural dimensions. Subsequently, practical indications for mediators will be given, that contribute to the broadening of the reader's own "cultural competence," so that s/he will be able to conduct an adequate mediation of the intercultural conflicts that s/he is to address.

In this book we speak of members of Western and Sub-Saharan cultures. Here we do not mean any national or regional cultures that we might understand fixedly and rigidly. We do not, therefore speak here of "the" Westerns and "the" Africans. Instead, we intend to take our point of departure in tendencies of cultural dimensions and orientations. This means that, when we speak of Western or African cultures or individuals, we understand the persons as being of a particular extraction, and tendential cultural orientations, who embody individual characteristics and are variable. It is in this sense, then, that we speak simply of "Western" or "African" persons.

We have selected the area of Western-African encounters on particular and special grounds. On the one hand, the cultural dimensions of Southern Africa evince a considerable difference from those of the West. This applies to how the persons in question deal with, among other things, time and space, gender roles, hierarchies, and styles of communication.

Furthermore, no publications on intercultural mediation are as yet to be found, in the literature that would have these cultural centers of gravity and this association. Again, our choice is founded on the culturally specific competencies of the authors and their long years of work in Southern Africa. Finally, one more motive for the publication of this book is to make it available to groups of mediators.

Demonstrably, competency in intercultural mediation can be acquired only when its so frequently described generalities are solidly anchored in a particular cultural region. For us, this is Southern Africa.

With this book, then. we should like to address persons who work in intercultural contexts, such as social pedagogues, social economists, social workers, psychologists, and, obviously, those groups of persons who work in such contexts as experts, managers, and in professional and leadership functions in international and multicultural teams. Likewise, may employees of foreign offices, who have to make political or administrative decisions on the fortunes of Africans, also consider themselves addressed here.

We wish all readers much delight in their studying, new knowledge for their own work, motivation for solving intercultural conflicts, and an enduring interest in the development of their own intercultural personalities, so necessary for the work of intercultural mediation.

The Authors
Dar-Es-Salaam / Cape Town

© Coesebrink 1995

1. Introduction

"Mediation," from the Latin *mediatio*, "division in the middle," is to be defined as a procedure for the resolution of conflicts through one or more "all-party third persons." Mediation has been practiced for several millennia, in the most diverse parts of the world. Even a quick trip across the globe shows the size of the historical contributions of mediation the world over.

This manner of intervention on the part of third parties, or mediation, is attested as early as the time of the great Chinese dynasties, in which it played an outstanding role in Chinese philosophy. Probably one of the most solid foundations of this fact is the long-standing tradition of Chinese value-orientations in terms of culture, harmony, consensus, and cooperation for Chinese philosophy, religion, and culture. This thinking finds a special place in the philosophy, and concept of philosophy, of Menzius (Chin., Me-Ti, 371-289 BCE), in which the creation of social harmony leads to a return to the harmony of nature, perceived as existing in full concord with itself. This understanding of philosophy has maintained its consequences for strategies of conflict-resolution down to the present day (Thomas/Schenk 2001).

In ancient Greece, as well, one of the principal cradles of our own cultural sphere, it is reported that, between the two urban centers of the country, Athens and Sparta, envoys repeatedly "ran their errands," as we might say, coursing back and forth between the two great cities. The role of "transmitter" or "go –between" was usually assumed by well-known personalities of smaller Greek cities, who would bear the words of one party to the other. They did not always "transmit" word for word, however. Instead, when necessary or useful, they "wrapped" them, diplomatically and rhetorically, in somewhat different words, lest the conflict escalate, so that peace would be endangered. This was a kind of political and economic mediation, which, in principle, we still know today.

In our own geographical environment, we likewise know of mediations from the time of the Middle Ages. Here, many priests are summoned to mediate budding conflicts—especially in families. In the framework of the churches, and faith communities, ecclesiastical mediators find fields of endeavor that they can closely link up with their chief calling. In Christian theology, as well as in Christianity as actually lived, Jesus is regarded as the Mediator between God and human beings. The Mother of Jesus Christ, Mary, is seen, in Catholic popular piety, as "Mediatrix," and highly revered. Today, as well, especially in rural communities, priests and pastors are found to be taking on the role of mediator after the exemplar of Jesus Christ. In many countries of the world, even to the present day, it is altogether expected that clergy fulfil the function of mediator in the widest range of occasions.

Since the sixties of the past century, there has been a great deal more mediation in the United States. There it is a procedure developed with definite rules and phases, introduced especially in community work, to resolve conflicts and contentions among neighbours, friends, and acquaintances more quickly, more effectively, and financially less expensively than in court procedures. In the wake of the peace and civil right movements, "Alternative Dispute Resolution," ADR, is developing, which includes mediation. Beginning with the notion that, in any case, it is the conflicting parties who, in principle, are the best agents of the resolution of their own conflicts, ADR represents the opinion that it is better to solve one's own conflicts than to hale them before a court.

In the 1980s, the "new wave of mediation" swept across Europe and Germany from the United States. Since then, the number of mediations conducted in everyday affairs has manifested a clear growth. Places for the formation of future mediators are full. Supply and demand are on the increase. In Western courts, where mediators are sought especially in divorce cases, places for appeal to court-like mediation procedures have multiplied.

In Asia, preponderantly in Japan and China, this has not been a matter of novelty for a long time. In both countries, mediators are regularly included in judicial procedures, to arbitrate between conflicting parties for the sake of maintaining harmony. The Asian "cultural circle" or milieu may well be the one today in which the most mediation in the world takes place.

However, we also know of mediation procedures from Southern Africa. Many ethnic groups are returning to traditional African forms of mediation. Here what is usually done is to call a popular or village assembly, in which one person assumes the role of mediator. The process of the mediation runs clearly differently from the Western. Besides, roles and positions are altogether differently defined from our own case. This kind of mediation, into which we enter in detail and ad hoc in chapters 4 and 5 is frequently dubbed "traditional mediation," or "ethno-mediation. Since these concepts are not used in a particularly value-free manner, and are often seen as "traditional," by contrast with "modern,: we should prefer to call this form of mediation "old African."

Just through these few examples, we see what an authenticated procedure mediation is for intervention in situations of conflict, and one that we observe as fundamental in many cultures and countries of the world. Frequently, these procedures were developed independently of one another, in conflicts, and thereby underlie culturally specific bases and characteristics. Therefore it is not in order to adopt a starting point in the notion that mediation "goes the same" in all the different cultures of the world. However, it can be assumed that there are conflicts throughout the world, and in all cultures. The path on which they are dealt with varies, however. Just as varying are the ways and manners in which conflicts show themselves, and how they are perceived and constructed, individually, as well as socially. Conflicts, accordingly, can be observed as a universal feature of our *conditio humana*, and they interconnect all persons. How persons in different cultural contexts express and reveal conflicts, however, and what kind of conflict resolution they prefer, must be considered in their specific cultures. This is undertaken in this book.

In our Western-style everyday understanding of conflicts, they predominantly appear rather negative, problematic, and critical. Human beings scarcely "suffer conflicts gladly," and even today most Western-style persons still see conflict as a burden, not necessarily as a chance for change. This understanding of conflict is owing, on the one hand, to the intensifying emotions that so often play a role, such as annoyance, anger, sadness, grief, shame, etc., at times all wrapped up in one. On the other hand, a rather negative attitude toward conflicts prevails also in the tradition of Western conflict theory. Only in recent theoretical approaches is conflict seen as something positive, as opportunity for transformation, as the chance for a change, for a positive shaping, and as the occasion of one's own broadening and personality development.

It is precisely this understanding of conflict that we should like here to lay as a foundation, for it indicates the way, in a new kind and manner, of dealing with conflict within one's own cultural group, as well as in situations of "cultural overlap" (Dadder 1987)

Now we should like to give readers a brief introduction to intercultural mediation.

It seems reasonable to us first to present the ideas and concepts of conflict, culture, inter-culturality, and intercultural mediation (see chap 2).

Subsequently, mediation as a concept of conflict solution in the Western sense will be elucidated. As a model, then, we shall thus indicate how mediation is taught and practiced today in Germany, along the guidelines of the Federal Union for Mediation, incorporated (see chap 3).

In reference to intercultural mediation, we shall present factors of cultural influence in and on the mediation process. Here the role of the mediator, the role of the conflicting parties, and phases and processes in intercultural mediation will be considered explicitly.. Further aspects, as, for example, emotions, gender roles, power imbalances through cultural influences, culturalization, the formation of stereotypes, and language will be studied. Finally, we shall take a look at the challenges and opportunities of intercultural mediation (chap. 4).

General statements on interculturality and the intercultural usually tend to mean, "All or nothing." Alongside this root, autobiographical roots can also become applicable (see Foreword). This will tend to occur when we consider the subject matter of interculturality in conflict and mediation, especially with an eye to Western and Old African concepts of mediation. Examples from the African cultural context can clarify cultural dimensions and factors of influence, as well as demonstrate culturally specific insights, and behavioral manners and attitudes in the area of conflict and conflict resolution (chap. 5).

In the final chapter (chap. 6), opportunities for sensitivization and training of mediators are presented, who work in intercultural and especially in African contexts. Here, centers of gravity are specified, on the development of intercultural competency, cultural reflection on self and foreigners, as well as the broadening of consciousness with an eye to cultural schemata, and to interaction with the culturally specific presentation of values.

By way of conclusion, examples will be given of simulations of intercultural mediation, with "roadmap," role descriptions, and information for mediators. These simulations are practical exercises, to be introduced in culturally heterogeneous, as also homogeneous, groups of mediators, who are in the process of formation and improvement in the area of intercultural mediation. They are useful in achieving a cultural-transcending consciousness and awareness, and they can thereby contribute to a definite elevation of the competencies exercised by mediators when dealing with persons in situations of intercultural conflict.

*When it is a matter of the event prophesied,
the prophesying is frequently the main thing.*
Thomas Hobbes

2. Introduction to the Assemblage of Conceptual Subjects

2.1 Culture, Inter-Culturality, and Values

As our intent in this book is to deal with intercultural mediation, it will be apposite first to clarify the concept of culture with which we work. Our premise is that the concept of culture that we define is fundamental for everything that follows here.

First of all, interdisciplinary discussions of the concept of culture seem very diffuse and diverse. Basic for a grasp of the key concepts of culture, interculturality, values, conflict, and mediation--both conceptually and with regard to content—seems to us, for reason both of its practicability and its timeliness, to be the approach taken in "constructivist philosophy." This approach, in the area of the sciences, and in the post-modern era, has found a growing number of convinced followers (Anderson 1983, Berger/Luckmann 1977/2000, Watzlawick 1985). We adopt it for the reason that, systematically, it allows room for perceptions and constructions of concepts and realities. In this approach, all persons, both as individuals and as members of society, have their own, unique eyes, with which they consider and (re-)create their reality. According to the constructionist view, persons encounter a wider dimension in intercultural contexts (cf. chap. 2.3). Thus, in intercultural contexts, there is already a multiplicity of relevant constructivisms. Accordingly, in situations of intercultural "overlapping," the dimension of a "foreign" cultural construct must be regarded as obligatory. To the observer, that which is the "other" thing or person does not seem as it seems to the other person. The contribution of interculturally competent persons consists in the recognition, and appropriate inclusion in interaction, of the effects of a foreign, albeit constructive, reality.

The concepts presented below, developed now systematically, now historically, are intended by us as a proposition to the readers of this book. The latter, for their part, may re-construct these "constructivistically" fashioned and presented concepts in accordance with their own interior perspective. The "is" assertions of this book, therefore, do not describe situations or conditions of the "objective" world. They present certain perceptions of the authors. Let us therefore begin with a definition, and the history, together, of the concept of culture—as we see them.

It is more than one-half century, now, since two anthropologists, A. L. Kroeber and C. Kluckhohn (1952), attempted to shed light on that field of definitions concerned with the concept of culture. As long ago as this, in the literature, they came upon 164 definitions of culture, whose multiplicity, in most cases, can be traced to the distinct finality--and to three fundamental directions taken in the definition of culture (those of Arnolds, Tylor, and Boas)--which today are still subsumed in most definitions of culture.

We wish to come to an adequate definition of culture, for purposes of this book, that will be theoretically and practically applicable. Here we have taken an orientation to ethnologist Franz Boas' apprehension: that every culture demonstrates particular traits of cultural diversity, while at the same time, and in parallel, introducing universalistic elements.

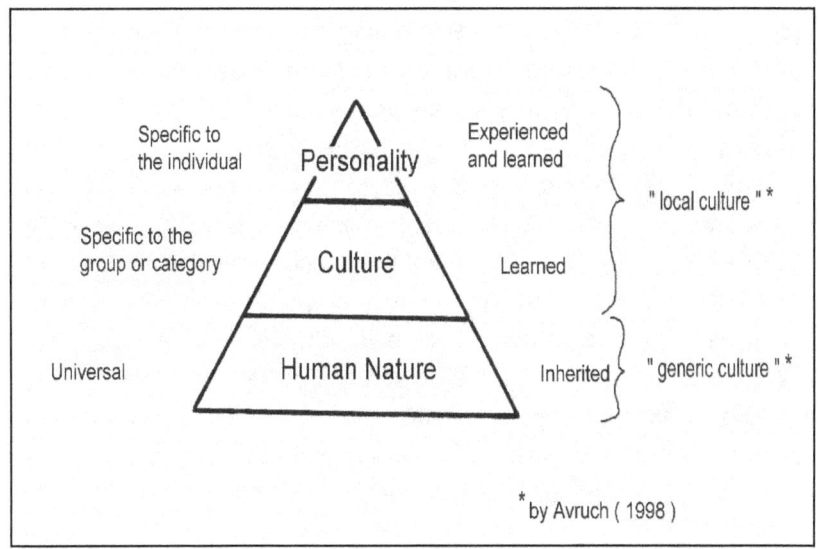

Graph: Levels of Influences on a Person

Avruch describes these two areas as "generic culture" on the one side, and "local culture" on the other. "Generic culture is a species-specific attribute of Homo Sapiens, an adoptive feature of our kind on this planet for at least a milliion years or so. Local cultures are the meanings created, shared and transmitted (socially inherited) by individuals in particular social groups."

"Generic culture" thereby contains universal attributes of human behavior and human nature, as, for example, the basic human needs. „Local culture," on the other hand, attracts attention rather to cultural diversity, differences, and particularism, that is, from a "culturally outsider" perspective on the communality of the "generic culture," and, therewith, of culture-transcending phenomena.

Once "generic culture" has been premised as fundamental, the concept of what Avruch calls "local culture" is in need of a closer examination. Hofstede takes a special interest in the definition of "local culture." In his conception, every human being bears within him/herself corresponding patterns of thinking, feeling, and possibilities for action, which s/he has learned in his or her cultural socialization—in the process of "enculturation." By analogy with this process, Dutch psychologist Geert Hofstede calls such patterns "mental programs," and the route of enculturation "software programming." A familiar concept for this "mental software" is "culture" (Hofstede 1993).

By way of "duplicating" the above, Hofstede now differentiates culture into two parts. The first is a visible part, which he designates "Culture I," and which comprehends the phenomena of everyday life in the world, as greeting, eating, "feelings," corporality, etc. On the other hand, there is, for Hofstede, "Culture II," always a rather less visible, collective phenomenon, that the person shares with the human beings who live in the same surroundings, that is, where this culture was learned. Here it is especially norms, values, the history of the communication community, and spatio-temporal orientations.

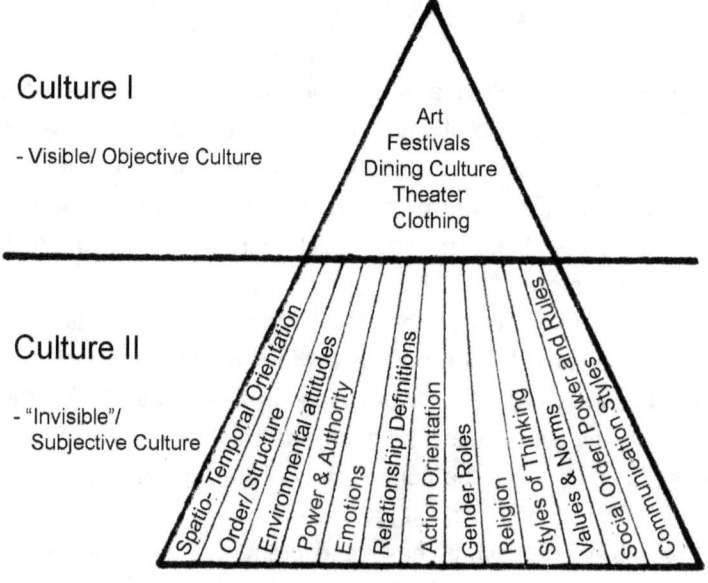

Graph: Iceberg Model of Culture

Edward T. Hall, in his *The Silent Language* (1959), was the first to record the concept of "intercultural communication." He defined intercultural communication as a communication between persons of different cultures. Here it is a matter of the exchange between persons of different cultural origin and diverse cultural groups. This exchange occurs when a person or persons from one culture come into interaction with one or several persons from another culture. Here the starting point is the fact that persons of diverse cultural extractions will demonstrate different attitudes, conceptions, and manners of perception and behavior. Only a few years ago, it was mainly diplomats, expatriates, and world travelers who dealt in intercultural questions. Nowadays, in the wake of globalization, and the multi-culturalization of societies, this phenomenon is no longer restricted to particular groups within a society. Be it at the supermarket, on the stair, or at school, we encounter persons with culturally specific traits everywhere, persons with differences—or similarities—in attitude, perception, and behavior. The question that now comes front and center, is, "How can human beings understand one another when they do not share common cultural experiences? Often, in situations of intercultural communication and interaction, irritations appear, and conflicts or clashes arise. Once you slip into such a situation in intercultural contexts, you will very probably not be able to get out of it.

We now define the question of interculturality in direct connection with the definition of culture proposed above: a situation is defined by us as intercultural when at least two persons meet communicatively and interactively. Thus, *per definitionem*, one of these two persons belongs to another culture than that of her or his vis-à-vis. Thus, the two persons are distinguished in their "local culture." Here, according to Hofstede, belong "Culture I," that includes the phenomena of the everyday world, and "Culture II," that, for intercultural mediation, comprises such important distinct value orientations as belong, *per definitionem*, surely, to cultural community, inasmuch as the latter makes common value systems and norms available--which, again, can be expressed in regulations in interaction, communication, and behavior. By way of the symbolical system called "speech," it becomes possible to share verbal meanings, and certain regulations, and, thereby, interpretations of schemata. The meanings of words are defined culturally, through a kind of cultural "grammar"--by a grammatical frame of rules, then, but one that is usually unconscious and implicit. This "grammar," like one's native language itself, is learned in the course of enculturation and socialization. It molds the mind as well as the body, in their attitudes and movements. In intercultural situations, this phenomenon often leads to irritations and misunderstandings.

Every culture, every cultural system, contains "cultural orientations" (Clyde Kluckhohn 1951). Under cultural orientations, those aspects are to be understood that attract attention, within a culture, to "attitudes toward and evaluations of culturally specific social behavior of human subjects" (Flechsig 2001). We here apply the concept "orientation," inasmuch as, in its quality as a social construct, it indicates that the patterns of perception and action of a person have been learned, and can at any time be subject to alterations. This is especially important in view of culturally specific behavior, and forms of the possibilities of change.

Cultural orientations, in the literature, are set on a par with value orientations, which lie at the basis of a cultural system. Florence Kluckhohn and Fred Stroebeck (1961) first applied the term "value orientation" as a key concept for the description of cultural variants. Here they refer to Clyde Kluckhohn's definition, as early as 1951, of "value orientations" as "a set of linked propositions embracing both value and existential elements." According to Flechsig (2001), this definition is closely connected with the question of whether, and to what extent, behaviors, attitudes, thinking, and emotions transcend culture, so that they are subject to general laws common to all persons, or whether such primary laws are culturally specific, and marked by cultural variation. The former position is designated under the concept of universalism, the latter under that of cultural relativism (cf. chap. 2.1).

In the cultural sciences, we see an image today that looks like this: the multiplicity of cultural orientations that occur in each culture, shaped with simple cultural specificity, can be grasped with the help of a limited series of categories or dimensions. In chapter 5, which is concerned with Western-African interactions, these cultural orientations are to be pursued concretely. For example:

- Communication
- Dealing with time and space
- Attitudes toward the environment
- Individualism and collectivism
- Order and structure
- Causal attribution
- Styles of thinking

Knowledge and consciousness of culture and value orientation, especially in respect of intercultural encounters, and of the development of intercultural competency in mediators and conflicting parties, play a great role, and therefore deserve special attention (cf. chaps. 5 and 6).

It is hoped that this book will indicate a route that will be seen as basic, and appropriate for operating in supportive and constructive manners, in intercultural mediation.

2.2 The Meaning and Importance of Conflict

In everyday life, it is very common to speak of conflicts, difficulties, or problems. We need only utter the word "conflict," to entertain the well-founded supposition that the persons around us produce associations similar to our own.

In Germany, it seems accepted, in broad parts of society, in principle, to speak of conflicts. In many areas it is even hoped that conflicts be addressed openly and honestly, with the aim of approaching them actively. Now, just what constitutes a "conflict" for a person, is difficult to define, even generally for Westerners. For many, the word: conflict" is bound up with violence or force, or with physical confrontations. For others, instead, it is psychic and cognitive confrontations that are at issue. Conflicts can be of an interpersonal or intra-personal kind, and appear as latent or manifest. When a conflict begins and when it ends is difficult to assess. Subjective traits play a large role here. We now make bold to look into this entire matter somewhat more deeply.

Different approaches even to the theory of conflict encounter the concept of "conflict" on the most diverse levels. Neither in the area of the social sciences, nor in the political and cultural sciences, has an all-comprehensive theory of conflict been developed to date. Rather, theoreticians from different disciplines and times refer to conflicts as partial aspects of their theories. This has occurred beginning with philosophy, and, proceeding through the political and social sciences, and psychology, to pedagogy and technology. Thus, models and theoretical approaches in the investigation of conflict exist, but without embedding in an all-inclusive theory of conflict. We have chosen a few of these theoretical approaches for presentation in the following paragraphs. They contain partly typologies of conflicts that are of importance for this book because they seek to systematize elements of a theory of conflict. These systematizations are intended to serve as a first orientation to, and "index" of, conflict. Here it will be helpful roughly to localize the core elements of conflict, thereupon to treat them in a certain order.

Now let us cast a brief glance at the perception and treatment of conflict in history and today.
In antiquity itself--in Heraclitus, the greatest philosopher of transformation, in Thucydides, and, before our calculation of time, in Chinese philosopher Me-ti--struggle and conflict were the subject of philosophical discourse. The writings that these philosophers produced figure as precursors of the political "realism" of the modern age.
In political realism, represented by philosopher Thomas Hobbes and theoretician of power Niccolo Machiavelli, conflict figures as negative, and as based either on destructive human impulses (Machiavelli), or, in Hobbes, on the particular kind of interpersonal

relations that the latter presents generally as bellicose: „Homo homini lupus" (Lat., „The human being, to the human being, is a wolf").

In the classical economics of the eighteenth century, the subject of conflict is taken up for the first time as social conflict, and, in David Ricardo and Adam Smith, considered in respect of anthropological „sociality" and motivation for action--this as always building on pursuit of interests. and on the satisfaction of needs. Here, conflict takes on a certain form of competition, nor one exclusively negative for society. On the contrary, both liberal economists teach that competion and conflict enrich a society as a whole.

A few decades later, philosopher of Western Idealism Georg Friedrich Hegel develops his dialectical theory of conflict. This finds an echo in the materialistic dialectic of Karl Marx and Friedrich Engels, which sees the history of hmanity as a history of class struggle.

In the nineteenth century, in various approaches, social Darwinism appears (e.g., Herbert Spencer), which understands conflict as a natural struggle for survival—the „survival of the fittest.." Here, later, ethnology and social biology come in, which conceive conflict first and foremost as a behavior led by instinct.

In the twentieth century, Konrad Lorenz traces human aggression to aspects of cultural history. To him, aggressions seem inborn behavioral tendencies, along with behavioral variations sparked by environmental stimuli. His student Irenäus Eibl-Eiblsfeld represents the thesis that wars are to be attributed to anthropological constants. According to Prätorius (1985), two viewpoints, especially, enter the foreground, that still indicate directions today. One direction is oriented toward Marx and Engels, and sees conflicts as increasingly an element of social politics, since they manifest themselves collectively. The other direction takes conflict as individual and biographical, and as, in its very approach, set over social stability, and the maintenance of the system. Georg Simmel (1992) introduces formal traits of conflictive relations into sociological theory, and analysis, and thus is often dubbed the first theoretician of conflict. He sees conflict as a form of {"societation," since conflicts, he holds, have been conducted through interactions that mold special life. Conflicts are positive, says Simmel, since they have been produced and formed through the individual rules of society, which have been contributed to the formation of societies. In Simmel's conflict functionalism, human conflict is researched from the perspective of its role in the preservation and transformation of social groups. In recent approaches of conflict theory, as well, within theories of social science or philosophical theories, conflicts are investigated from the perspective of their role in the preservation and transformation of social groups. In recent approaches of conflict theory, as well--within theories of social science, or philosophical theories or, for example, Habermas (1981), Luhmann (1987), Bourdieu (1982), Honneth (1994),and Lytard (1987)-- conflict figures as a constructive or positive potential in societies.

Only since the fifties of the twentieth century has what is generally understood under conflict theories been included in the process of conflict development, or included in the confrontation with emotions in the conflict, along with the de-escalation and ascription of conflict (Augsburger 1992, Daily 1991, Ricci 1980). In recent times, attention has been given to the conflict-models that sketch a general and universal appeal: Erich Weede (1986) and Hubert Blalock (1989). Here, social conflict is ascribed a "eu-functional" effect. Basically, the questions of the origin of conflict and its meaning for society are therefore of interest.

Let us now look into the connection between an understanding of conflict, and of mediation. The foundation of any mediation is the conflict at hand. Without conflict, no mediation. With this in mind, let us now consider, in a systematic view, what conflict means in our connection. Here we ought to adduce the original, etymological meaning. The syllables of the compound verb confligere (Lat.), on the one hand, as a transitive verb--on the level of activity--correspond to the English "crash together," or "collide." On the other hand, as an intransitive verb, they describe a condition or structure that may be translated as "being 'at' each other," "being in struggle." With this double meaning, it is interesting that the original form of the verb itself indicates an active and a passive semantic. These two meaning-forms point to the distinct backgrounds of a conflict to be investigated in a mediation. Before we turn to mediation, however, let us look once more at the phenomenon of intercultural conflict.

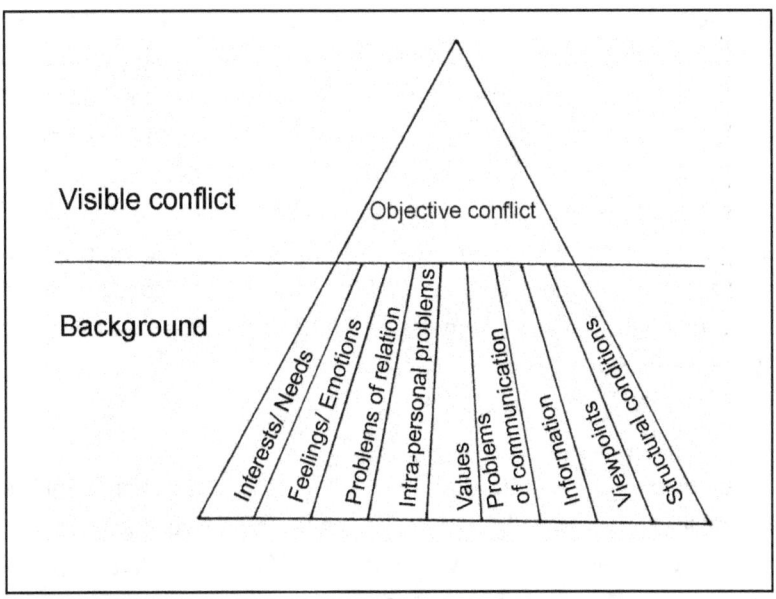

Graph: Iceberg Model of Conflict (Besemer 1999)

2.3 Conflicts in Intercultural Contexts—a Question of Realities?

Conflicts—as already mentioned—seem to us to consist of constructs of reality, that manifest themselves in the individual, in society, and in culture. This is expressed especially in intercultural conflicts.

Frequently, in the literature on conflicts and conflict resolution, cultural aspects are left out of account. A universality of conflicts, and the possibilities of their solution, is postulated transculturally. Further, it is assumed that Western models of conflict resolution are so adaptable that they can level out any cultural differences that may be at hand. In this direction, culturally adapted techniques of conflict resolution that have been researched are simply added to the repertoire of techniques of conflict solution available—or else previous intercultural training is scheduled, in order to be able to insert a cultural sensitivity into the conflict and the process of conflict resolution. Thus, intercultural training is often seen in the current literature as an „adjunct module" for the solution of intercultural conflict. However, whether this provides the most favorable avenue for dealing with conflicts is questionable. For us, the situation seems, instead, to be that, not only in the conflict itself, but also in the mediation of an intercultural conflict, a new, qualitatively different form of conflict and conflict resolution is constructed, that integrates intercultural competencies and generates an intercultural synergic effect.

Let us now cross over to what Lederach (1`988) says about conflicts in intercultural contexts.[1] [[[See below, under chap. 2, for footnote.]]] For him, they are an opportunity to perceive different realities: „Conflict situations are those unique episodes when we explicitly recognize the existence of multiple realities and negotiate the creation of a common meaning."

Here, conflict is the confrontation or collision of distinct realities and value concepts in a context of multiple possibilities of perception, that call for development in the light of the conflict. For the development and understanding of intercultural conflicts, Lederach develops a „conflict framework."

It contains three principal elements:
- Conflict is to be seen as a process of long duration, manifested.
- An adequate, descriptive language will be needed in order to understand the conflict and transform it.
- The conflict must be regarded critically, in order to perceive its diverse realities, and to render them indeed "realistic."

The point of departure is the assumption that conflicts are natural, and that they arise in all of the relationships and cultures of the world. Thus, holds Lederach, conflicts are socio-culturally constructed facts actively created through the interaction of the participants. Here we see the essential dialectic of situations of conflict, as it is experienced in the construction of any social reality—in the sense of Berger and Luckmann (2000). In conflicts, then, it is a matter of the quest for, or the development of, a common discovery of meaning. This interactive process of a common discovery of meaning, holds Lederach, is anchored in the roots of perceptions, interpretations, possibilities of expression, and intentions. Thus, culture is composed of common deposits of wisdom, and of schemata, which schemata, again,
- schema of expression
- schema of perception
- schema of interpretation
- schema of intention

is tightly molded around "social reality." It is assembled, Lederach continues, of networks of subjective realities having (culturally defined) collective meaning (Lederach 1988).

If we begin with the notion that the evolution of the individual's socio-cultural identity, and subjective experience, flows by way of ever-recurring cycles of consent, confusion, conflict, and enlightenment, then conflict cannot just be whittled away by consciousness- training and "sensitization." Rather, in connection with the learning of and acquaintance with "social realities" and their meaning, conflict can be handled in (acc. to Watzlawick 1978), and through, communication.

David W. Augsburger (1992) like Lederach, describes the conflict as a crisis, which instructs human beings that there are manifold realities, and that they frequently have to be managed as common realities. Each situation of conflict, writes Lederach, consists of histories of various parties, histories frequently opposing one another, together yielding a single history, with roles and positions held by all persons concerned. In intercultural conflicts, there is a further difficulty. It lies in the fact that culture contains an empirical order--through speech, perceptual schemata, techniques, values, and hierarchical structures--in which activities and emotions have space and limits for freedom of movement and power of imagination. According to Augsburger (1992), intercultural conflicts exist in the tension between "the same thing and the other," which can take on diverse behavioral shapes:

- The same thing controls and reduces the other.
- The same thing subordinates and exploits the other.
- The same thing destroys the other and, where possible, denies that it is doing so.
- The same thing excludes the other and flees the threat of the other.

Confrontation in terms of conflicts and conflictive situations is also very closely bound up with core cultural values and their roots. Conflicts afford a profound insight into the social reconstruction of the reality of a culture. If situations of conflict be explored, they can show that human beings live under manifold frames of reference and circumstances at once, and that thereby they experience multiple realities. In conflicts of social interactions, these manifold realities must be coordinated, and connections drawn between them.

In its essence, accordingly, conflict is a special type of reality, which must be recognized as such, and calls again and again for new definitions of its multiple realities and encounters. Here, according to Augsburger, (1992, pp. 16ff.), clashes may arise, when there are different underlying definitions, and mutual understandings simply are not stipulated.

Let us summarize. Conflicts are shaped universally, culturally, and individually. They occur everywhere in the world, are culturally marked, and are experienced individually. Behavioral manners in conflict are culturally specific, since every culture builds itself its own repertoires of conflictive behaviors, hierarchies of value, and conceptualizations of lawfulness. Thus, there is always a wide spectrum of habits, personal styles of communication, and ways of behavior, which do not necessarily make generalizations easy. The borders of the spectrum, again, be they social, emotional, legal, are defined by the culture and by one's own conceptualizations of values. Every individual, every group and society, have value conceptualizations, hierarchically ordered and solicited. Furthermore, individual values always stand in connection with socio-cultural. Precisely in conflicts, these values standing a complex, dynamic process with one another.

The following steps of analysis are available, according to Augsburger (1992) for the analysis of situations of conflict and value conceptualizations that transcend cultures:

- Where does the conflict occur? (Context)
- Why does it occur? (Basis/Causes)
- What is the attitude or stance, and activity, of those involved, vis-à-vis the conflict? (Values)
- How is the conflict and conflict-resolution dealt with? (Attitudes and engagements)
- What patterns of behavior are employed in the conflict? (Behavior and emotions) What styles of communication influence behavior in the conflict?

Further, it is important to recognize whether, in the view of those involved, it is a matter of a constructive or destructive conflict. With a constructive conflict, the individuals or groups are in a position to define it, to work out its focus, to visualize and formulate it. The exact causes of the conflict can be established without the introduction of further, secondary potential for conflict. Still, confidence is necessary in the effectiveness of the process of conflict resolution, and interest in a cooperative solution of the conflict.

If the conflict has a destructive direction, the conflictive topics, the self-justification, the negative attitudes become extended, and far removed from the actual cause of the conflict. Finally it is no longer a question of the original conflict. Instead, other matters inject themselves. The conflict escalates into the areas of strategies of power and menace, coercion, deception, and betrayal. Frequently, opinions become polarized, anger grows, and narrowed, selective perception begins to interfere. Especially in relation to social conflicts, extreme escalation can occur, not always without a violent course.

In the following chapters, let us seek a constructive approach to escalation in intercultural conflicts.

3. Introduction to Mediation in the Western Context
3.1 What is Mediation?

Let us begin with what is familiar to us: with the philosophy and basic principles of Western mediation. The Western mediation procedure is oriented to certain basic principles, phases, and techniques, and defines the role of the mediators in a way and manner specific to our culture. We must now consider these points more closely.

Mediation, as we know it in Europe today, is a procedure for the resolution of conflict through an "all-party third party." As already mentioned, "mediation" denotes a "middling," and refers to mediation in cases of strife and conflict. The mediating third party endeavours to be of assistance to the conflicting parties in their search for an agreeable solution to their problem. This solution should, for one thing, be seen to have been found by the parties themselves—the mediators simply supporting the path to the finding of this solution—and for another, mean a victory for all involved. This principle of a "victory on all sides" is also called the win-win principle. The goal of the mediation, then, is to find a "win-win solution." This means a resolution of the problem that will be satisfactory to the majority of those concerned, in all parties to the conflict, or at least provide the most satisfying elements of an optimal solution. This solution, with which both parties can win, follows an altogether determinate principle. Mediators do not look for a resolution to the problem on the level of the positions taken by the parties on a the same day. Instead, they attempt to "get behind" the positions presented by the conflicting party, and to bring out and "work" the interests that stand behind the conflict. After all, one frequently finds that the interests of the conflicting parties while distinct, and different, are not mutually exclusive! Here, after a mere examination of interests, and the recognition that it is not a matter of mutually exclusive interests, new possibilities for a solution emerge. A classic example, repeatedly cited, is the conflict over the oranges, in which two parties wrangle over a single orange. Both are stubborn in their position: they need the orange, and that's it! However, after the interests have been clarified, it emerges that the one party needs the orange peel, in order to quarter it and use it for a decoration in a kitchen. What the other party needs, instead, turns out to be the rest of the orange, in order to squeeze it for juice. Suddenly, obviously, a "mediative" resolution is at hand.

Often, conflicts of interest fail to be solved because resources are available only in a certain quantity, and all parties stubbornly adhere to their positions without attending to underlying interests. Then, a compromise is struck, a partial solution, that frequently leaves both parties less than completely satisfied. In the example of the orange, a so-called compromise might stipulate that each party receive one half of the orange. There should be no question of such a compromise in mediation. Instead, it should be a matter of the "win-win" principle.

A mediation process provides a framework and a setting, in which the parties of the conflict can express their interests, and be supported in this by the mediator. In the Western process of mediation, there are certain fundamental rules and principles that we should now like to identify.

- Doubtless the most fundamental principle of mediation is willingness. Every person must participate in the procedure freely and willingly, otherwise the reluctant party will find it impossible to be completely engaged in the process.
- The fundamental rules to be followed in the procedure are discussed with the parties, and established in common. The basic rules that ought to be adopted in any mediation process are the following.
- The parties to the conflict speak in the first person singular.
- Each person allows the other to finish he or she has intended to say.
- No rudeness (verbal, nonverbal, physical) is tolerated.
- The procedure is confidential, and should be handled in a confidential manner.

- (. . .)
- (. . .)

If the parties wish to have other rules as well, these can likewise be discussed and adopted.

- A basic, and important, rule is also that the procedure must be kept confidential. This means that, outside of the mediation process itself, the mediators must not speak of the content of the mediation. Among the participants, as well, the question of confidentiality has to be posed. The parties decide in common how they will proceed with confidentiality. Here it will be determined whether other persons may be taken into the confidence of the individual parties, or whether the parties will decide not to reveal content and outcomes outside the process.

With reference to the solutions to be developed, the parties will be personally responsible for the solutions in their conflict. They know the series of problems best, and so can best decide how to report the solutions. Mediators provide the framework for a constructive solution. Their task consists in supporting the procedure, seeing that the rules are observed, and guaranteeing all parties the same opportunity of presentation and self-engagement. Furthermore, they help the parties to express their feelings and needs, and to listen to and register those of the opposite party. Next, they review the feasibility of the suggested solutions with the parties to the conflict, and record the conflict's final solution. This record can be written or oral. Here the important thing is simply that mediators make all participants aware of the binding force of this solution.

- The mediators must be neutral. This means that the third party must avoid "taking sides" through "conveyance," identification, or projection. Internal address or preferences regarding the parties, on the other hand, are divided amongst all parties simultaneously.

In this manner, the parties are accepted by the mediators and feel understood. After all, if an imbalance among the conflicting parties is reinforced by a partisanship on the part of the mediators, the process threatens not to arrive at a win-win solution.

- According to Marshall Rosenberg, the principle of non-violent communication can frequently be of a help, both to the conflicting parties and to the mediators. In this approach, it is important that emotions and needs be expressed. In mediation, this occurs, for example, from the side of the conflicting parties. However, feelings and needs must also be listened to. This occurs in the mediation, by the mediators, and subsequently by the parties to the conflict, with the help of a switch in perspective. This principle of non-violent communication is not applicable in the mediation process perforce. To be sure, it can be a support and help for all concerned to form the process as constructively and non-violently as possible, and to create an atmosphere in which all feel equally accepted, and think in a fashion oriented to a resolution (cf. chap. 3,5).

- Mediation is not a procedure that could replace therapeutic and juridical procedures. But it does offer a good opportunity to complement these procedures.

In sum, it can be said, with Dulabaum (1998), that the following four "A"s ought to find attention and consideration

All-party position	Empathy for all participants
Acceptance	Respect and acceptance for all positions and attitudes of all conflicting parties
Acknowledgment	Respect and acknowledgement for the positions and attitudes of all of the conflicting parties, with inclusive trust and confidence in their own solutions
Affirmation	Support and encouragement of the parties to the conflict in the expression of their own feelings and emotions, their needs, and their interests

Graph: The four A's

3.2 Areas of Application of Mediation

Now that we have briefly examined the process of mediation, it is important to explain in what areas of application mediation is usually introduced in Germany today.

The classic case of mediation is divorce. In some courts nowadays, the opportunity already exists of explaining the divorce procedure in court, with mediators, and thereby of obviating an actual judicial procedure. This "trial-like" explanation can also concern itself with, for instance, disputes over an inheritance.

Mediations are often introduced into conflicts between neighbourhoods, or city-quarters, that have had to be designated social "hot spots." The same holds for city quarters heavily marked multi-culturally. Here, it is persons of different cultural extraction who can often be helped by the services of "go-betweens." Among foreign authorities and offices, as well, at intercultural youth meetings, or social establishments, which are active in the area of intercultural work, additional qualifications in the area of mediation are required on the part of collaborators. Be it in the retirement home, the hospital, or public transportation, conflicts are present in organizations and in everyday living, and here intercultural components play an ever greater role.

Political mediation, as well, in a local, a regional, and especially an international framework, are familiar to us, not least of all from television. Repeatedly, for example, attempts are made to intervene between Israel and Palestine. Repeatedly, one hears of conflicts between minorities and states, in which mediations are conducted by outside mediators. The United Nations, as well, in its Charter (Article 33) provides for mediation as one of the various methods for resolving a conflict (Besemer 1999). Here the political area, naturally, includes local projects and citizens' initiatives, not least of all when environmental projects or trade policies are concerned.

A large number of mediations are likewise conducted in (international) economic work. More and more, cultural questions play a role, and it is no novelty in the daily life of companies when firms link in "joint ventures," or multicultural teams. The process is also introduced in disputes over renting and leasing.

Finally, a broader area that is now spreading in Germany is the area of school mediation. Here, mediation is conducted between students and teachers, teachers and teachers, and students and students. In many schools, there are already peer-mediation and student pilot programs in which students are trained to settle conflicts among fellow students themselves, by mediation.

3.3 What Is the Course of the Mediation Process?

Clearly the mediation process in Germany is structured according to the Western exemplar used in the United States. Grob divides it into an antecedent phase, a phase of mediation, and a phase of resolution.

The antecedent phase consists primarily of preparatory conversations with both of the particular parties of the conflict, if both have an interest in the mediation. Often, the situation is such that only one of the parties is interested in the mediation. Many times, however, the situation is such that only one of the parties has an active interest in solving the conflict by mediation. This party then turns to the mediator. In such a case, the mediator is often asked to address the other party and "get them on the boat" to mediation, to attain a participation by all involved. The antecedent phase can be very helpful in urging the process and in explaining the procedure. First contact with the conflicting party is, as a rule, decisive. It is an opportunity to create a pleasant atmosphere in advance, in order to guarantee a basis for a confident and trusting cooperation. In most cases, the preliminary conversation likewise serves, on the one hand, to clarify the questions that the conflicting parties may have, and on the other, for the mediator, for a first acquaintance with the series of problems.

Next begins the phase of mediation. This will be introduced, by the mediator, with a greeting and a (repeated) presentation of the procedure. A trustful atmosphere is created, the rules of conversation are laid down, and questions are explained.

After the introductory phase, the phase of presentation of the conflict is introduced. Here the mediator asks the parties to the conflict to present the conflict from their own viewpoint. In this phase, the parties normally speak to mediators, who listen actively, and in a given case pose questions of comprehension.

If the most important points, for each party, in the conflict are visualized on a flipchart and retained, the problem points are addressed in the phase of clarification of the conflict. This phase is preponderantly marked by the conflicting parties' feelings and needs being in the foreground. Here a special role is played by the interests that lie in the background, behind the positions. Now hardened positions are softened, and a common basis of deeper understanding is generated. It is in this phase what is in order is the application of "non-violent communication" in Dr. Marshall Rosenberg's sense (chap. 3.5). Now the parties begin to listen to each other actively, and once more to communicate otherwise than only through the mediators.

Once all points of conflict have been worked out, the process can be advanced to the phase of resolution. Desires and wishes, and suggestions for a solution, can be creatively shaped, on the basis of the preceding phases. Now they can be worked out in an orientation to outcome, and goal-directedness. All suggestions for realization are received, and verified in terms of their potential for realization. The examination of this potential is ordinarily undertaken with the help of the applicable SMART model (according to Filner and O'Brian in Ripke 1999), as follows.

Specific

The agreement should specifically determine who is to do what, and when, and how.

Measurable

The agreement should be apprehended positively, objectively verifiably, and in terms of its feasibility.

Acceptable

The agreement should be acceptable to the parties. That is, its content should be available to their full and entire production and realization.

Accommodated to Reality

This means that the agreement has considered all obstacles to realization.

Terminated

The phase of realization is terminated precisely. In juridical matters: the contract should define the time-spans allowed for the fulfilment of each contractual stipulation. Thus, even a mediation contract should specify a time limit for its execution, and the partners to the contract should know when the mutual obligations have been discharged.

Graph: SMART-Modell

After the conclusion of the phase of resolution, an arrangement can be formulated between the parties of the conflict. This is often done in written form, according to the SMART model.

Once the process of mediation has been brought to a close with an accord and agreement, the parties can seek to transfer the content of the agreement to daily life. A terminal point is specified, between the mediators and the parties, when the entire process can be completed with a conversation and assessment of the outcome. If, in the phase of application or conversation of assessment, it emerges that, in a given case, the agreement between the parties has not solved all problems, or one or other party remains unsatisfied with something in the agreement, or in its application, then the agreement must be reviewed. This can most often be done in the form of "Revisions of Agreement," although at times all must be begun over again, "from scratch."

> **Phases of Mediation: Overview**
>
> **Antecedent Phase**
> Mutual acquaintance and motivations for participation
> Preliminary conversation with the parties
> Preparation of the mediators
>
> **Phase of Mediation**
> Introduction
> Presentation of conflict by individual parties
> Elucidation or clarification of the conflict, in terms of feelings or emotions, needs, and interests
> Resolution of the conflict
> Reconciliation
>
> **Phase of Application**
> Test of the reconciliation in everyday life
> Conversation on the reconciliation, with assessment and, possibly, revision

Graph: Phases of Mediation

3.4 Techniques of Mediation

Mediators have various methods and techniques available that they can introduce into the several phases of mediation, in differentiated fashion. At this point we should like to present a few frequently applied techniques, and discuss them somewhat more precisely. Subsequently we offer a table, summarily cataloguing the techniques that are in general use. Owing to its importance, the concept of non-violent communication will be developed separately, in terms of Dr. Marshall Rosenberg's presentation.

Reflecting (Mirroring)

The technique of mirroring has the purpose of correctly repeating and emphasizing, on the objective plane and level, the episodes that are expressed, by the parties of the conflict, especially in the phase of presentation of the conflict. What was observed, heard, perceived? What evaluations were joined with these episodes and facts of the case? In a word, the mirroring technique has the function, for the triangle of the parties of the conflict "A + B" and the mediator "C," of making transparent, for all involved, the facts of the case now expressed and selected in perspective.

Active Listening

Active listening means an empathetic listening, in which one tries to understand what the other person feels and would like to bring to expression. Where I feel understood and accepted, I need not constantly repeat what I think, so that I am now more ready to listen to the other side as well.

The discharge of feelings and emotions with the help of this technique opens up a substantial vision of the parties' attitude and stance with regard to the points of conflict. The parties will not only feel themselves better understood, but, over and above this, will become clearer on their own feelings. Active listening encourages "saying more." The conversation can gain depth, and the things to be recounted will become less "emotional."

Active listening in no way means that, as mediator, one necessarily shares the opinion being articulated! It is only a matter of the correct understanding and "repetition," that is, the "reflection" of what is being said, as well as of the meanings of the articulated, of the articulator, and of his or her feelings and emotions. It is also a matter of "lingering" on the other, and on her or his perspective, and certainly of intentionally leaving one's own cognitive and affective thought schemata out of consideration. Accordingly, certain valuable rules speak of:

- presenting the other's viewpoint tersely and concisely, in succinct form,
- perceiving the other's facts and feelings,
- and not introducing any evaluations of one's own

Reframing

Reframing means that negative statements introduced by the conflicting parties in a given case are reformulated positively. The mediators give the statement a new "frame," as it were. If depreciatory, insulting, or provocative declarations are made, they can be reformulated and reshaped by the mediators into neutral and acceptable, positive statements. The starting assumption is that a positive core always stands within the depreciatory declaration. This core is then is "peeled," laid open, by the reframing..

This technique's effectiveness consists in a transformation of the conversational atmosphere, destroyed by negative and offensive statements, into a positive, constructive one. Openness, and mutual acknowledgment, promote a readiness for effective cooperation in the process of mediation.

"I" Statements

The conflicting parties are required to speak exclusively in "I" statements, and not, as readily occurs in conflictive situations, in "you" statements. "I" statements mean that one speaks only for oneself, speaking of what one experiences oneself, or what one does, and what emotions are personally connected with it for oneself. The application of "I" statements is intended to bring it about that a higher degree of self-awareness is intended by reason of the fact that one "names" only oneself, and thereby expresses oneself understandably and concretely.

Every person speaking for her/himself accepts at the same time responsibility for her own acting, and no longer speaks in generalizations and abstract expressions. This implies that one need not feel offended by one's vis-à-vis. "I" expressions renounce direct attacks on the "you," and this across the board.

Doubling

Doubling is a method that can be applied when mediators have the sensation that persons cannot express what they actually would like to express. Even in conversational situations in which difficulties arise in direct communication between the parties to the conflict, the mediator can "double" one side or the other. Especially in intercultural situations in which language barriers might play a role, the method of doubling is particularly indicated.

The mediator first ascertains with the conflicting parties whether s/he may double the one or the other. In case of consent by both sides, the mediator now speaks in the place of the person(s) in question, thereby doubling her/him/them, and speaks in the place of that party, empathetically, and in the first person singular—"I." The mediator adopts, as it were, the role of the corresponding party. In many instances, through the introduction of "non-violent communication," "I" statements, and reframing, doubling can produce a more pleasing atmosphere, a de-escalation, and a clarification of viewpoints. When the doubling is over, the mediator ascertains with the conflicting parties the degree of accuracy of the doubled words and content. If the doubled party is not entirely in agreement, that party may correct, supplement/complement, or reformulate what has been said. If the doubling has been accurate, then the party being doubled can attempt once more to repeat what has been said, and now fit it out in her/his/their its own words. The difference between doubling and active listening lies in the fact that the mediator applies "I" language instead of "you" language, and that the conversation is laid out in the form of a dialogue.

We should now like to present the fundamental techniques of mediation in the form of a table. We have entered those techniques more expressly of which we conclude that they assume a special function and effect in intercultural mediation. (Of this, however, we shall speak in chapters 4 and 5.) In the following table, you will find that we characterize all of the fundamental techniques:

Technique	Content/Purpose in course
Mirroring	Taking up words and content
Active Listening	Noticing needs and feelings behind the words
Reframing	Turn negative words in positive words
"I" Statements	One speaks for oneself
Doubling	Speaking for one person
Non-violent Communication	Communicating observation, feelings and emotions, needs, and wishes
Inquiring and concretising	Go into detail
Praising	Expressing recognition/acknowledgment
Forming syntheses	Undertaking association of discrete elements, working out communalities
Echoing	Emphasizing words
Paradoxical intervention	Reinforcing the negative
Initiating changes of perspective	Listening to the other side
Formulating metaphors	Formulating graphic transferences or figures

Applying analogies	Introduction of respectively similar expressions
Drawing up hypotheses	Expressing suppositions
Condensing sequential material	Condensing longer units of address
Allowing individuals to speak	Allowing room for individuals
Conducting brainstorming	Permitting creativity and associations
Body language and bodily expressions	Wholly perceiving, grasping, and formulating nonverbal communication
Techniques of inquiry	Posing purposeful questions (open/closed)
Creating frameworks and atmosphere	Opening up words and gestures

Graph: Techniques of Mediation

3.5 Non-violent Communication (NVC) according to Marshall Rosenberg

Non-violent communication (NVC) was developed by American psychologist Dr. Marshall Rosenberg. On the one hand, it is a method, a technique, for communicating in an altogether special way, a non-violent way. At the same time, it is a person's philosophy, attitude toward life, and inner disposition. The method of non-violent communication can help in situations in daily life, catalysing human intercourse in the direction of positive confrontations. Especially, it offers a tool for conflict mediation, providing a situation in which one confronts the other in a positive and constructive manner. It enables the subject to "hear me out," and to get at the positive core of a statement or proposition. It is a principle of philosophy that, behind any statement ever encountered, howsoever negative in form that statement may be, stand feelings, emotions, and needs that seek to be brought to expression.

It is one of the purposes of non-violent confrontation, therefore, to recognize and expose these needs and feelings. In the phase of clarification, the point is to work out feelings and needs as the deep foundation of a conflict. Thus, NVC here finds special opportunities of application.

In case a person is unready, or not in a position, personally to express herself or himself "non-violently," then the mediators will assist, from time to time, in "reframing" what has been said, in the model of the NVC.

Representatives and users of the NVC model start out with the hypothesis that this form of communication releases positive energies among persons, and that these energies enrich and broaden life.

When human beings communicate their own feelings, emotions, and needs—instead of hiding behind "positions"—they thereby connect with the feelings and needs of their respective vis-à-vis.

This form of receipt of linkage, that on the most profound level—the level of emotions and needs—makes possible, among human beings, an exchange stamped by openness and empathy. Marshall Rosenberg speaks for a universalistic attitude," whose point of departure is that everyone in the world has needs and feelings. When these are expressed, and received by the other, they can offer the basis of a constructive and non-violent communication. Here the meaning and importance of non-violent communication reach a greater intensity. It is here that human beings have the capacity to join together on the deepest level, that of human nature, as represented by "generic culture" in the form of anthropological universals (cf. chap. 2.1). If this stamp or "coinage" is the same for all human beings, then the basis, the origin, stands forth of a communication transcending the cultural boundaries of "local culture."

Below, we briefly present the-four-step model of non-violent communication. according to Rosenberg (2001). Since it is a theoretical model, one cannot assume that all steps will flow perfectly, in the same series, in everyday situations. Instead, the model, with its phases, must be adapted to the respective elements of communicative praxis.

Speaker's Perspective	Listener's Perspective
Observation	**Observation**
Honestly saying "How I'm doing" without reproaches or criticism	Empathetically accepting how you actually are, without listening to reproaches or criticism:
The concrete actions that I observe (see, hear, recall, imagine) and that contribute to my well-being: "When I (see, hear)…"	The concrete actions that you observe (see, hear, recall, imagine) that contribute to your well-being: "As you have (seen, heard) . . . ."
Feelings	**Feelings**
How I feel in connection with these actions:	How do you feel in connection with these actions?
"I feel (I am). . . "	"Did you feel . . . ?"
Needs	**Needs**
Life energy, in the form of needs, values, wishes, expectations, and thoughts, through which my feelings and emotions are generated	Life energy, in the form of needs, values, wishes, expectations, and thoughts, through which my feelings and emotions are generated
Because I . . . (need, would be glad to have, desire, hold as important, fondly regard . . .) . . ."	Because I . . . (need, would be glad to have, desire, hold as important, fondly regard . . .) . . ."
Requests	**Requests**
Clearly, as far as request is concerned, what enriches my life requires—without demanding	Empathetically to accept, without demanding, what would enrich your life, without listening to a demand
The concrete actions which I should like to have ("get") performed: "And would you please . . . ."	The concrete actions which I should like to have performed: "And would you mind if I . . . ?

Graph: NVC

We shall treat the model of non-violent communication again later, more precisely, with a view to intercultural communication between Westerns and Africans.

3.4   The Role of the Mediator

In principle, mediations can be conducted by one person or by a team of mediators. Whether the mediation is conducted in a team is often a matter of expense. If complex and long drawn-out mediation procedures are expected, or group mediations, it may be well-advised to work with a team of mediators in order to conduct mediation in these conflicts. In many conflicts, and especially often with divorce and marriage, it is helpful to work in a team of mixed gender. The supposition here is that membership in a trans-gender team will exclude problems bound up with only one of the sexes. Thus, each of the sexes has its special dialogue partner.

Oftentimes, however, even in group mediation, it will be of advantage if both sexes are represented on the mediation team, since the gender perspective emphasizes different aspects.

For a positive approach to the conflict, it is important that the team be accepted and respected on the side of the partners to the conflict. The team is one of trustworthy and reliable persons, who are expected to bring appropriate and adequate competencies to the mediation. As already mentioned, the impartiality of the mediators is presupposed. They should not be "neutral," or "party-less," but advocates of all parties. This means that they will deal with everyone involved with empathy and understanding, and be prepared to understand sympathetically all that is said. They will not seek to evaluate or criticize, or pass judgment or condemn. Just so, mediators are independent of interest in the events of the conflict, since they themselves bring no interests of their own into the conflict. They simply provide the framework for constructive conversation on the conflict, without determining the process as to its content. In this way, the parties' own content can be "refereed," if mediators are helpers in the expression of emotions, needs, and interests. If parties meet in conflict that stand in different positions of power or authority, mediators attempt to equalize these imbalances intentionally. This can occur by way of a "consciousness-raising" of the parties regarding the imbalances (e.g., between parents and children), or by way of certain intentional arrangements (e.g., between managers and employees) (cf. chap. 4.6.7).

From the roles of the mediators as here described, it emerges that the latter do introduce certain fundamental and attitudes. They bind themselves to an ethical self-understanding:

- They endorse an optimistic image of the human being.
- They supply a frame for fair processes of explication.
- They accept the criticism of the conflicting parties.
- They show empathy and tolerance in confrontations.
- They exclude their own interests from the mediation; otherwise they are seen as "caught."
- They indicate the possibilities and boundaries of the mediation.
- They attend to the full transparency of all steps in the mediation.
- They bind themselves to confidence.
- They esteem and respect the parties in their differentiation.
- They encourage the parties to take responsibility.
- They "take their time," and are patient.
- They use as neutral a language and speech as possible.
- They try to see to it that both parties in the process "win," lest the outcome be "zero to zero."

Now that we have laid the groundwork for an understanding of mediation in the Western context, we should like to take a closer look at the element of the intercultural in the mediation process.

4. Introduction to Intercultural Mediation

4.1 Application to a Third Person

Turning to a third person is a long-established means of interpersonal communication. It is designated by the term, "triangulation." Especially when it is a matter of conflictive areas, or their resolution, third persons may be introduced as, for example, mediators, legal advocates, arbitrators, elder statesmen, or friends. We know this not only from our own cultural milieu, but also from the experience of negotiations between states, and in dealings with ethno-political conflicts (cf. Ropers 1995).

Augsburger (1992) observes that, precisely in the "Third World," the most frequently used method of conflict-transformation passes by way of a third person. In the Western World, however, continues Augsburger, in the former Soviet Union and in Eastern Europe, the tendency exists to select direct confrontation and negotiation. Here, he says, at least two parties (A/B), and a subject matter, are always implicitly represented. This constellation of two parties and a subject to be addressed are a "triangular situation." If a third party is introduced, then the process may come to include the formation of a coalition with one of the parties. A triangle (ABX) would arise, this author continues, if both parties (AB) were to be interested both in the relationship obtaining between them, and in the subject of the conflict, and their attitudes were all of equal weight. However, there would also be different emotions or attitudes concerning X, so that tensions and conflictive experiences would promptly appear. Augsburger holds that the manner of resolving these tensions will vary from culture to culture.

What is mediated in conflicts, and where and by whom they are mediated, is bound up with culture, and depends on cultural expectations that vary precisely interculturally.

4.2 What is Intercultural Mediation?

There are various ways to approach intercultural mediation. The designation, "intercultural mediation," can be misunderstood. One might assume that it is a matter of specific methods that would be particularly appropriate for dealing with intercultural, ethnic, or international conflicts. However, this is not the case. There no longer exists a method exclusively suited for addressing intercultural conflicts. The concept of intercultural mediation is frequently applied on three distinct levels. We should like to present these here.

On the one hand, intercultural mediation can be understood as constituting a variant of mediation among individuals, groups, or states bearing diverse cultural traits. In such a case, we are dealing with mediation in intercultural contexts. That would simply mean that a Western process of mediation could be used in contexts of mediation among persons of various intercultural contexts. In Western cultures, mediation is marked by the Western process of mediation, while in Asian or African cultures, for example, mediation will be based on processes specifically adapted to the particular culture.

For us—in our Western context—the basis on which the method of mediation will proceed will be that already developed in chapter three. This regards the proposed techniques, phases, and "setting" of the mediation, as well as the role of the mediator.

Accordingly, intercultural mediation is distinguished from the "normal" Western mediation process on the following points: the mediators, and the conflicting parties, can proceed neither on the basis of a reference to identical or similar cultural value-orientations, nor on that of mediation procedures of a Western character. A consequence of this is that both the formal side of the procedure of mediation, and the content-side of the negotiations, must be dealt with in ways different from the methods usually followed in intra-cultural settings. If one's point of departure in a situation of intercultural mediation is that the participants have at least an identical cultural basis of values--varying only individually—then this basis must be addressed anew, in intercultural situations, and differently with regard to the conflict and the procedure of conflict solution. Thus, a principal task of the mediators will be to develop and propose different as well as common value-orientations, and culturally specific philosophies with their foundations and regulations, in order that they may become conscious, and be fruitfully introduced into the process.

On the other hand, the concept of intercultural mediation can also represent "traditional" mediation, or "ethno-mediation," as applied in the current literature on extra-European forms of mediation (Augsburger 1992). In this case, it is a matter of a process of mediation from a culture other than Western. Here, Western culture does not present the framework upon which the whole procedure is built. Rather, what we have is a culturally specific mediation setting, which will define the following areas in a culturally specific manner:

- The underlying philosophy, and basic principles, with their values-orientation
- Course and order of the phases of the mediation
- Techniques of the mediation
- Conduct of conversation and style of communication
- Role of the mediators
- Role of the partners to the conflict

Augsburger (1992:204) has set the Western model, which he calls the North American, over against the non-Western, which he calls the traditional model. As for a selection of culturally differing points, he calls attention to certain Western distinctions in the following table:

North-American Model	Traditional Model
Formal process, with specialized roles, in the context of certainty and stability, as well as of constructive goal-orientation. Time and space are clearly defined.	Mediation as task of the community, with inclusion of qualified leadership personalities. Usual structures and information flow are incorporated into the procedure. Time frames and context are incorporated for the sake of social interaction.
Direct communication is desirable. Rules of communication & speaking. Process structured and directed through the mediator with direct confrontation and communication styles.	Indirect, informal third-party processes are preferred to face-saving, minimal threat, and to a balancing of relations of power, as well as of differing linguistic and rhetorical abilities. Communication can also pass through other persons, as, e.g., family members. Thus, there are often several participants among the parties to the conflict.
Time is linear (monochronic). Strict time schedule. "One after the other" and "One thing at a time".	Time is relational (polychronic). Time schedules, and relations to second-rank participants; therefore the individual explanations follow the rules of the social rituals.
Structured process, orientated to tasks and outcome Autonomy and individuality of the parties stand at midpoint	The process is directed to the relaxation of tensions in the society/community. Reconciliation stands at midpoint.

Mediators as technical specialists stand in impersonal relationship with the parties. Accords are contractually regulated. After the end of the mediation, no further contact between conflict partners and mediation.	Mediators as leadership personalities for the community and the social context. Therefore a personal incorporation into the social network. Relations are continued after resolution of the conflict.

It seems to us, however, that the conceptual opposition or comparison of the North American model with the traditional model is problematic. Here it is suggested that, apart from the specified North American model, there would be basically a traditional model in other cultural regions of our world.

Furthermore, most readers associate "North American" with "Western and modern," many even with "progressive." This alone makes for a perspective that we cannot share. In such a case, the notion of "traditional" is demeaned, as it would now represent only a backward form of culturally exotic mediation processes.

As in chapter 5, we shall extensively replace the problematic concept of "traditional" with the concrete designation of the cultural region, as, for instance, old Indian, old Chinese, or, in our case, old African.

The adjectival attribute of "old" defines not opposition to "modern," or "new," but simply indicates the fundamental fact that, in large "cultural circles" of this world, as in Sub-Saharan Africa, there are procedures of mediation that have been handed down for millennia. These procedures were conceived, constructed, and introduced long before the "American model" or the "Western model" entered the scene.

But let us now turn to the third level of intercultural mediation: the **culture-synergetic model of mediation**. Finally, with intercultural mediation, an altogether new form of intercultural mediation can arise, one of situational adaptation, and acceptance by the participants. Markedly at play here are the synergy effects of elements of various traditions of mediation. Synergy, in this connection, means that the respective elements of parts of one's own culture are taken up, in a spontaneous process, and woven together with parts, or all, of other cultural contexts, into an entirely new culture of mediation. Consequently, it is a matter of a process of re-construction of the intercultural mediation, one having its own quality. We shall find an example of this reconstruction process in chapter 5.

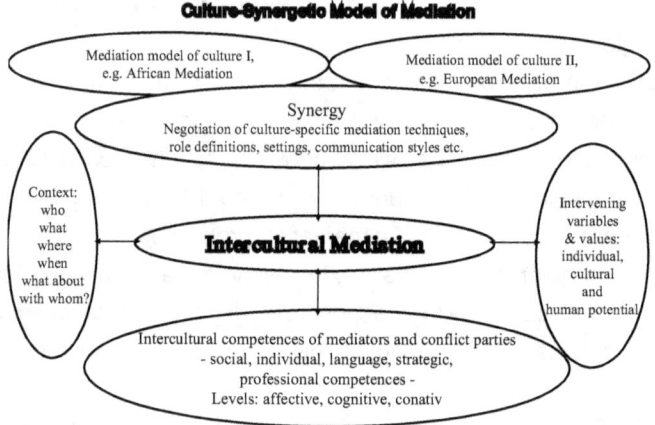

Graph: Culture-Synergetic Model of Mediation (Mayer 2005)

By way of example, if a Western-African mediation is conducted in Western cultural contexts, then the setting of the Western mediation process lies at the foundation. Then it will be in order to offer respectively open spaces and open times for options, in order to introduce African elements of mediation. If, on the contrary, the intercultural mediation takes place in cultural contexts of Southern Africa, then it is probable that the manner of mediation prevailing there, will form the framework in which a creative process of intercultural mediation will unfold and develop, into which flow elements of Western mediation.

In the present chapter, we address intercultural mediation in Western and other intercultural contexts. In chapter 5, on the other hand, we shall concern ourselves with intercultural mediation in the sense of African mediation and synergistic intercultural mediation.

4.3 Areas of Approach in Intercultural Mediation

With the ever-increasing proportion of foreigners in the Western Federal Republic, the potential for intercultural conflict is on the rise. This potential for conflict is clustered in the following selected areas, in which mediations are being conducted in the context of the respective culture as well.

- Intercultural conflict in urban quarters
- Intercultural conflict in the area of pedagogy, especially in transferring between schools or with foreign visitors
- Intercultural conflicts in the dispatch of delegations to foreign countries
- Conflicts in businesses and factories using an intercultural or international work force
- Conflicts in businesses with joint ventures and mergers
- Conflicts in social institutions, as in hospitals, enterprises for youth, associations, churches
- Intercultural conflicts in government and private offices, state organizations
- Conflicts in bicultural marriages and families

4.4 Dealing with Western Techniques in Intercultural Mediation

Basically, we need not fear being very far off the mark if we assume that many Western mediators work with the tools of Western techniques in mediation even in intercultural contexts. As to the success and effectiveness of these techniques in intercultural contexts, however, we must make certain distinctions. First of all, Western techniques are effective only in a limited number of the world's various interregional cultures. In other words, what is applicable in Southern Africa may be evinced as counterproductive in Asia.

Conversely, there are culturally specific Asian or African techniques that will simply not be understood in the framework of our Western techniques. These techniques from other cultural regions have found application for centuries, of course, in their culturally specific contexts of mediation,

Let us now briefly and succinctly consider and examine the techniques with which we have already become familiar in chapter 4. Here our main focus should be on the regional center of gravity of Southern Africa.

It is true that reflecting, and active listening, as well as echoing, may be possible in the regional cultures of Western and Southern Africa without the arousal of culturally specific irritations. It may be, however, that, in other regional cultures, as for example in parts of Asia, the repetition of what has already been recounted will be regarded as impolite, since members of these cultures may think that they have not been correctly heard, and that their vis-à-vis may be seeking to correct them through another vocabulary even when it is the same content that is at issue.

Another consideration is that of the explicitly expressed feelings and needs addressed by active listening. Every culture has its own concept of the proper manner of dealing with the expression of emotions, and this to the point that certain feelings of aversion or anger must be so controlled as scarcely to be intelligible and interpretable by members of another culture. To the extent that it may be possible, this problem of the management and expression of emotions is therefore to be explained in the foreground of a mediation.

The technique of reframing is positively distinct from other, "problematizing," techniques, since it enjoys a general, and very broad, familiarization in the cultural world. With high probability, therefore, it is applicable in all cultural mediations. In many black African ethnic groups of Southern Africa, for example, it is typical of socialization when, in contexts of communication, persons value an emphasis on the positive side of a "negative" perception or "negative" message. Africans, in addressing a problem, frequently utilize the expression of emotions and needs of their own—feelings and needs implied by the problem for themselves. Only in extremely rare instances is the problem itself expressed explicitly. This frees the situation of communication, in a confrontation on a given matter of dispute, from pressure—what in the West is called nonviolent confrontation.

"Chair your own meeting" is a basic principle of the culture of group conversation. It comes to us from the United States, and has found entry into the process of mediation. Individuals ought to speak only for themselves. In most cultures of a collective orientation (see chap. 5), this principle is irrelevant. On the contrary: when someone sounds the word "I," it is assumed that s/he is raising herself above the relational group from which she comes. At the same time, it may be that, by employing the first person, the agent of discourse is actually rendering the views of the "we-group," without explicitly stating this. It frequently occurs that the parties of a conversation who come from another culture than the Western, express themselves in the "we-form" in order to suggest their membership in a culture actually participating in the conversation, even though their family or cultural group may be in no way involved in the mediation. The "we" stands for "I."

Thus, the mediator's polite indication that s/he will be speaking in the first person plural has a different meaning in mediation, and one that ought to be explained in advance, in terms of the culturally specific usage of the parties in the conflict.

The technique of duplication, in an intercultural framework, is likewise to be introduced cautiously, since it is not easy to foresee what this technique may occasion with members of other cultures. Frequently, in the Western mediational connection, duplication ought to be introduced prudently, since it can occasion the arousal of powerful emotions. Furthermore, it is true that, through the process of duplication, persons not easily using formal conversation can be assisted in their expression by the proffer of words from another mouth. Nevertheless a question is to be asked: can a mediator actually reach the needs and feelings of a person of a different cultural character, and, accordingly, repeat them, in the individual case? Thus, even though this technique can be put to use in the intercultural area, the attempt ought to be made only after an engaging explanation of the culturally specific manners of its uses and effects, as well as after a confrontation with the respective, culturally specific, backgrounds of the parties of the conflict.

Finally, we should like to indicate the fact that the technique of the paradoxical intervention, in which a participant enunciates and "defends" the negative counterpart of his or her position, is to be introduced in the intercultural area only with the most extreme caution. Even the mediator's positing of direct hypotheses, as well as the direct addressing and formulation of corporeal expressions, should be utilized with care. Last but not least, this caution is indicated by the fact that bodily expression is culturally specific, and, accordingly, can be interpreted in a culturally specific way. Besides, the bodily expression of the partners of the conflict in intercultural mediation ought not to be undertaken by mediators whose formation is Western, because nonverbal expression occasionally falls into culturally specific zones of taboo.

Other techniques, as, for example, the formulation of metaphors or analogies, can have a very positive effect on the process (cf. chap. 5.6.2), if they are applied in a manner compatible with the culture in question.

4.5 The Role of the Mediator in Intercultural Mediation

Thus, when we address our attention to mediation in intercultural contexts understanding it as intercultural mediation on the first level (cf. chap. 4.2), in the Western connection the foundation would probably be that of Western mediation.

First, interest in a solution to the conflict is established on the part of all participants. Here, as well, an even-handedness is to be expected on the part of the mediators. They seek to acquire information concerning the conflict, and to render it transparent for all involved. The intent is that the communication of the conflicting partners be supported in such a way that, when it comes to perspective, each side will understand the other, and a dialogue on the problem fields—including emotions and needs--can become possible.

It is of great importance for intercultural mediation that the mediators be conscious of their own prejudices,, stereotypes, and value-orientations. Only when this is the case will it be possible to adhere to a high degree of even-handedness and acceptance vis-à-vis the conflicting partners. Simultaneously, the mediators in intercultural mediations are responsible for exposing prejudices, stereotypes, and cultural values on the part of the conflicting parties as well. Accordingly, the phase of the illumination of the conflict acquires an altogether special position, often lasting appreciably longer in intercultural than in intra-cultural processes. This is founded on the fact that a cultural reflection on self and others of all participants is tied in with process, and that this leads to an increased "cultural sensitivity." Processes of intercultural mediation often only offer the partners to the conflict an entry into this area. The area of cultural "sensitivization" offers mediators a good training opportunity for learning to appreciate the culture factor in the process, and for becoming experts in cultural phenomena themselves. This can occur along various routes. Thus, mediators can gather culturally specific items of knowledge with reference to the parties of the conflict. This can be concerning books, professional personnel, or intercultural training. Further, intercultural training can be visited, so that the degree of one's personal intercultural competence is raised, and one's perception "whetted." This can occur by way of trans-cultural, general training, or by particular, culturally specific training (cf. chap. 6.3).

Furthermore, certain issues can be developed in working with the parties themselves--issues that emerge from the influence of culturally specific phenomena in the process of conflict and explanation. This can eliminate uncertainties, and obviate misunderstandings. Thus, culture factors must be repeatedly included in all phases of the mediation, from the introductory conversation to the final summary. Since intercultural mediation posits a special profile of demands on the role and function of mediators, it is useful for them to gain the support of persons familiar with the culture of the mediators, as well as with that of the parties to the conflict. These so-called bicultural persons can be introduced into the process of mediation either as informants on the culture in question, or as supervisors with regard to the culture factor. The "bi-culturals" thus engaged secure space for the mediators in which to consider and "play through" both the culturally specific phenomena with which they propose to deal, and with their opportunities when it comes to their own behavior. Then, if bicultural persons are included more intimately in the mediation process, they figure as "cultural conveyors"; now their principal function consists in offering reassurance to the respective conflicting parties in the course of the mediation. This reassurance essentially strengthens the conflicting parties, so that they become able to communicate emotions and needs without limiting their communication by cultural boundaries.

A principal problem that mediators must very probably pose themselves in intercultural mediations is the particular kind of underlying power inequalities at hand. It behooves them to make note of these, and balance them out. Power imbalances are often signalized in altogether different dimensions than in intra-cultural mediations (cf. chaps. 4.6,7 and 5.6,2)

Finally, it remains to be indicated that, in intercultural mediations, mediators' flexibility is particularly required. It would presumably be counterproductive were mediators to cling to experience of a Western character. On the contrary, it is to be expected that, together, mediators and conflicting parties should generate new systems substantially more complex than the Western model.

4.6 Challenges in Situations of Intercultural Mediation

Intercultural conflicts and situations of mediation indicate difficulties with respect to styles of conflict, the issue, and the solution. Further challenges can be ascertained in matters such as culturalization, prejudices, stereotypes, imbalances of power, and mechanisms of escalation in intercultural conflict. These situations and challenges will now be addressed.

4.6.1 Styles of Conflict

It can frequently eventuate that the culture factor be simply underestimated, or left unregarded. For this reason, certain patterns of attitude, behavior, or thought may not be completely understood by the mediators or by the other party to the conflict. Here it may be that the participants have no knowledge or experience with culturally conditioned styles of conflict. The styles of conflict maintained by one's vis-à-vis may not be specifically perceived culturally. Here, a mechanical "doubling" may occur of a person's personally and individually conditioned behaviors. These may tend to be culturally rather than individually conditioned. Now the participants may receive a different image of their counterparts of the other party than ought to be available in this artificially constructed cultural reality.

Here we wish briefly to present, from Augsburger and then from Bennet, two models concerned with styles of conflictive behaviors and of resolution. Both approaches rest on data collected worldwide, and their results are categorized from a universalistic perspective. Since these categories betray such a broad extension, both approaches presumably cover their object in all of its variants worldwide. The conceptual premise consists in each culture being normatively oriented to at least one category.

First we shall present Augsburger's model (1992), and then that of Bennett (1995). These models are prioritized in Augsburger's intercultural discussion, and surely exert the strongest current influence on the practice of intercultural mediation and communication, where discussion is on intercultural theory. Despite the differences in their approaches, these models can both become fruitful for intercultural mediation. They represent usable work hypotheses for mediators in intercultural contexts.

Augsburger's model demonstrates the variants that prevail with individuals and groups in conflict. Here it is a matter of conceptualizations, and behavioral variants, as they are more or less preferred in given cultures. Thus, we now present culture-transcending styles of conflictive behavior.

According to Augsburger, the most frequently applied strategy in the world is the avoidance of conflict. The Swahili even have a proverb, "Silence produces peace, peace produces safety." When conflicts cannot be avoided, the tendency all over the world is to conceal conflicts or to be quiet about them, and then to transform them into convertible strategies. In many cultures, persons are conscious that a deeper level underlies superficial, visible conflicts.

Culture-Transcending Options in Situations of Conflict	Description
Avoidance	The conflict is often dlissembled or denied. It can also occur, however, that other operations shift to the foregroud, such as ignorance regarding the conflict, or overlooking the conflict.
Repression	The open conflict is displaced, by the introduction of operations for the suppression of the conflict.
Displacement	The conflict is shifted, by guidiing it to another subject or party.
Management	The conflict is limited and restricted to a particular kind and manner, or its intensity is diminished through a mutual undertaking.
Resolution	The conflict is defined by alteration, that modify the cause or the impellling forces.
Utilization	The conflict is utilized, to construcrt new values and goal constellations, and to aim at creative transformation.

Graph: Culture-Transcending Options in Situations of Conflict

In connection with the various styles of conflict, we must include the gesture of forgiveness. Confrontation with the various culturally connected conflictive styles in intercultural mediation includes forms of pardon as a goal, since many societies accord forgiveness a very high respect. Three forms of pardon can be distinguished here: "punitive forgiveness," "inclusive forgiveness," and "reconciliatory forgiveness." The first enters the scene when forgiveness is besought out of fear of punishment. In the second, the driving force is fear of the withdrawal of love, which is supposed to resolve the tension and promote acceptance. The third is forgiveness that transforms a relationship. Here the very person and position is considered from another perspective, and altered, so that a forgiveness can be possible by way of insight (Augsburger 1992).

Applied to the role of the mediator in intercultural contexts, the table gives indications of individual and group postures in conflicts. The mediator is hereby in a position, by way of the application of specific techniques, to carry the process mediation further. By way of example, as soon as s/he remarks a behavioral option by one of the parties, s/he can "check" whether this option is conditioned by a specific culture, or, individually "joining in," can her/himself develop procedural options in the mediation and take appropriate steps.

After culture-transcending manners of conflictive conduct have been presented, culture-transcending styles of conflict solution should be developed. Bennett (1995) observes five intercultural styles for the management and resolution of situations of conflict: (1) denial/suppression, (2) power/authority, (3) third-person intermediation, (4) group consensus, and (5) direct discussion. Following Bennett, we should now like to set up a short table of these culture-transcending styles.

Culture-Transcending Style of Conflict Resolution	Description of the Style in Terms of "Interculturality"
Denial/Suppression	Resolution of the problem materializes through denial of the conflict Differences are downplayed, to preserve harmony
Power/Authority	Problem resolution materializes through the intervention of a recognized authority, such as a court, a majority decision, a person of authority, etc.
Third-Person Intermediation	A third person, seen as representing all parties, is introduced as arbitrator or mediator, to act as "go-between" among the parties to the conflict
Group Consensus	A committee develops ideas for a resolution of the conflict, and presents these as their decision. The entire group ratifies the decision.
Direct Discussion	The individuals involved in the conflict speak openly with one another concerning the conflict Account is taken of the perceptions, emotions, and positions of individuals

Graph: Culture-Transcending Style of Conflict Resolution

Here Bennett offers a useful tool: categories, according to which mediators can determine, in intercultural contexts, what style of conflict resolution is preferred by the parties to the conflict. Here again it is a matter of culturally specific tendencies. For example, the Shambaa in Tanzania take their orientation from "mediation" and "group consensus" as primary options in conflict solution, while our own reference is more probably to "direct discussion" or "authority," depending on the case. When the mediators in intercultural mediation know of such culturally specific preferences, they can better "thematize" and adapt the operation of the cultural styles to the behavior of the individual.

4.6.2 Mechanisms of Conflict Resolution and Models of Conflict-Solving

As we consider the process of mediation, we see that it can happen that mechanisms of conflict resolution recognized in the West are regarded as universal, and thus be just as presumably present in a person of a different cultural background. This would have the result that cultural characteristics and culturally specific marks would either not be recognized as such, in addressing conflicts, and be perceived and interpreted otherwise, or even simply not be taken into consideration. When there is an awareness of the existence of culturally specific approaches to mediation, the opportunity arises to "thematize" the process itself, and to lay open--to cite examples--the event and its procedure, the constitution of conversational rules, and the definition of conflicting parties.

It can occur that the very presentation of rules for the intercultural proceedings become the first negotiations on the common communications-structure. That is, it can occur that parties to the conflict take the notion to discuss the formal or informal character of the process of mediation, or that deeper discussions of the manner of written or verbal agreements must be found before that agreement can be addressed. Difficulties may emerge, if, on grounds of an assumed interculturality, models of conflict resolution are adjusted by the mediators without it being desired by the conflicting parties, or worked out in common with them.

Besides, the assumption that any and all cultural differences at hand can be adjusted by changing the model of conflict resolution is purely and simply erroneous. In this case, the alteration of the process of mediation, and the cultural adaptation of the setting, do not have the desired effect. By way of example, if techniques of conflict resolution are integrated into the Western process of mediation from other cultural areas, annoyance may easily arise with respect to the entire mediation process. Things stand otherwise, however, when new—even culturally specific—manners of procedure appear from the mediation process itself. In such a case, this creative process can have a very positive effect on the entire course of things, and contribute to the success of the mediation.

4.6.3 Culturalization

Just oppositely from an under-valuation of the cultural factor, it is likewise possible to overestimate problems in intercultural connections, and thereby to culturalize them. The culture factor would then be "over-interpreted" as the decisive factor. In view of the cultural factor, all other factors playing a role in the conflict would be interpreted in terms of the cultural factor. Thus the perception of culture, and possibly of culturally conditioned manners of behavior or thinking, would, in the case of a culturalization, dominate the entire situation. An example of a culturalization would be, if an African and a German sought to resolve a conflict through mediation, and the German always insinuated to the African that s/he must, after all, prefer a mediation for the resolution of the conflict, since all Africans had rather settle the conflict indirectly, or by way of third persons, than do so in direct discussion (cf. chap. 4.6.1). In this case, the German would have used prejudice as a strategy vis-à-vis the African, and left the other factors in the background.

A cultural phenomenon ascribed to an entire group, and then to an individual person belonging to that group, is the earmark of the process of culturalization. Altogether closely bound up with processes of culturalization, then, is the—often unconscious—conception that persons belonging to a particular national group, and thereby possessing a national membership, become representatives of the said national culture, or even (to factor by the next higher exponent) vehicles of the assumed stereotypes and prejudices of this national culture. A conflict occurring between members of different national cultures need not always be an intercultural conflict. The probability is higher, however, that it is indeed a matter of an intercultural conflict when two persons of distinct national origin enter into conflict, and it emerges that, for example, one of the persons belongs to a religious group originating in the Asian cultural space. If it comes to a clash between these fictitious parties, in which each represents the respective values of her or his respective religions, and insists upon them, then culture plays the following role: the values-orientations transmitted through the Asian religious form come to clash with the values of the other party. A "culturally indexed" conflict of constellation of values is in the offing.

These examples make it clear that the culture factor can be very diversely understood, and that a person's national appurtenance is not unconditionally decisive for an intercultural conflict, although it can be such. At this point, the extent is investigated to which differences or communalities between the parties are in agreement with their membership in their respective national cultures, and can be explained by this membership. When these different manners of thinking, behaving, and relating influence the process of the working out of the conflict in decisive form, then such a conflict can be called an intercultural conflict.

4.6.4 Prejudices and Stereotypes

Classically, psychology, social psychology and sociology deal with research in prejudices and stereotypes. Only in recent decades has the direction of this research gained importance with respect to intercultural contexts in "social relations" or "social anthropology."

The concept of prejudice is essentially defined by its normative, moral content. Accordingly, prejudices are distinguished from other conceptualizations not by way of inner qualities, but through their social undesirability. Prejudices, then, are only social judgments that clash with acknowledged human, and culturally defined, value concepts. Prejudices frequently emerge by precipitous judgments without a more exact knowledge of the matter at hand (Lat.., praejudicium, "precipitant decision"), as well as by way of a stubbornness in clinging to these judgments. Thus, frequently, prejudices are not disarmed by counter-arguments. At the same time, prejudices arise through generalizations from individual cases, or experiences of individual cases. Allport (1954) defines prejudices with respect to ethnic groups as "an antipathy based on a faulty and inflexible generalization. It may be felt or expressed. It may be directed toward a group as a whole, or toward an individual because he (or she) is a member of that group." According to Gudykunst (1991), prejudices are "natural," and unavoidable, and inherited through the socialization of one's own group. Here all persons—to a particular individual degree in each—is the vehicle of positive and negative stereotypes. As a tendency, persons usually join positive prejudices to their own group (the "in-group"), and negative prejudices toward other groups ("out-groups"), or, instead, just the reverse.

Stereotypes, like prejudices, are unavoidable, and "natural." They are a result of social categorizations---that is, images of social categories used by persons to categorize and systematize their environment. Stereotypes, then, are generalizations arising through cognitive processes of systematization, and have their principal function in the simplification and reduction of contingencies. Accordingly, they serve for the simplification of the cognitive or behaviorally relevant adaptations necessary for the development of complex connections and pieces of information communicated to a person by the environment.

As pluri-dimensional images, stereotypes vary in their complexity, their specificity, their favorable disposition, and their individual and cultural validity. Here, the tendency exists that the degree of association with membership in a given group, and with individual psychological attributes, will be very highly regarded. When a person ascribes certain stereotypic schemata to a certain group, then the moment she or he speaks with a person of that group, the communication and the process of the relaying of information is influenced with greater security and certitude. Furthermore, stereotypic expectations are created as to how an individual of a given cultural group will behave. With the automatic ascription of one's own stereotypic attributes to this particular cultural group, the perception of one's neighbor also changes: the observer now sees of this neighbor only what the former has already accumulated in terms of a stereotype of the latter's cultural group. Then, if the neighbor behaves otherwise than expected, frequently these behavioral manners are experienced and interpreted in terms of one's own stereotypes. Thus the stereotypes already at hand reemphasize the neighbor's manners of communication and behavior, in the sense of a self-confirming kind and manner, and so become a kind of "self-fulfilling prophecy" (cf. Watzlawick 2001). The reality created through one's own stereotypes thus repeatedly corroborates itself, in individual contact with the members of the socio-cultural group in question, and so once more receives the habitual perception of its group-specific life traits.

For situations of intercultural mediation, this means that reciprocal prejudices and stereotypes must be laid open, and become conscious, in order not to disturb the communications process and place the procedure of resolution in danger. If the intent is to achieve a relativization of the negative effect of prejudices, it can be assumed that the limited time available in a meditation process is probably altogether insufficient here. Techniques of mediation like reframing, concretization, and detailed investigation, supply a useful toolbox, with whose help prejudices can become visible, and stereotypes can be most readily discovered.

4.6.5 Culture as a Strategy

In situations of mediation in which the conflicting participants are of differing cultural origin, it may occur that culture be introduced strategically. In such a case, the culture factor is consciously or unconsciously utilized to direct the negotiation to the pleasure of the respective parties. All of those involved are thereby confident that there cultural differences, but no one can say exactly at what point there really are cultural differences, or is it only that certain other things are being emphasized. Liebe (1996) observes: "True, cultural differences are objectively given; but at the same time, they are still accompanied by the aura of the nebulous. It is impossible for outsiders to review their real relevance. However, they maintain a potential for astonishing 'turns' in intercultural discussion or negotiations.

Where culture is introduced as a strategy, it is usually a matter of culture difference being emphasized. Simultaneously, in that case, it is implicitly explained that no real agreement is possible, since the parties to the conflict are so different. In principle, this argument, standing in the background, can then give each party a hiding place, if it seems appropriate to them to interrupt or break off communication, to shape the process destructively, to maneuver themselves out of a given situation, or to alter a situation to their own tastes.

In such a case, mediators are asked to acknowledge this state of affairs, to communicate its presence and nature, and, together ith the conflicting parties, to deal with it accordingly.

4.6.6 Emotions

A "cultural dealing" with conflicts and their solutions is also greatly diversified if it addresses fundamental cultural values, along with the culturally specific emotions connected with these.

According to Rosenberg (1990), emotions are what in "folk ethno-psychology" are described as "feelings." Here, the primary feelings are defined, in number and content, differently by different authors.

However, the lists usually include joy, fear, sorrow, anger, and disgust as fundamentally and universally adopted. Nevertheless, all authors are in agreement on the point that, on the one hand it is only a limited number of primary feelings, and on the other hand that experiences of feelings consist of a synthesis of the feelings in question and a cognitive achievement.

For an appraisal of the place and functions of emotions in intercultural mediations, recent comparative research in psychology and ethnology is of special relevance.

Emotions in Western societies are often explained in terms of psycho-biological structures, and considered as distinct from ratio. At the same time, they are ascribed to a person's individual aspects. But emotions in other cultures tend to be set in the context of interpersonal relations. "Emotional meaning is then a saocial rather than an individual achievement—an emergent product of social life" (Lutz 1988).The complex meaning of emotions can thus stand in strong correlation to cultural values and social relations. Emotions can express cultural value, or construct them.

In the area of research in emotions, ethnology concerns itself with emphasis on and analysis of culturally specific, emotional manners of behavior and their cultural specificity or universality. One direction taken in ethnology can relate to the assumption that there are culture-transcendent, fundamental emotions. The other direction "regards emotions as culturally constituted cognitive constructs" (Röttger-Rössler 1997).

Both directions, however, are in basic agreement that emotions betray culturally specific definitions. In different cultures, then, identical words can contain or induce different experiences and content as a background. Especially, however, feelings can implicitly reflect cultural values (cf. Lutz 1988). Methodically, concepts of emotions can be unlocked most and directly by way of language, which means by way of the vocabulary of emotions.

Rosaldo's (1984) point of departure is that thoughts and feelings are not the same. Rather, a decisive role is played by the fact "that feeling is forever given shape though thought, and that thought is laden with emotional meaning." In these terms, emotions offer a road to the recognition that the social world is one I which the human being is involved. Concretely, this means that emotions express themselves in social practices and histories in which the person plays too, and which the person recounts. And so, feeling is always dependent on how the transpired is understand, and which reactions are constituted on the strength of that. To make emotions and their functional concepts useful in situations of life and of the everyday, and useful for the mediation process, Shweder (1991) poses the following questions:

- What data lie before us in our consideration of emotions? (Taxonomic question)
- Which situations evoke which emotions? (Ecological question)
- What do feelings imply? (Semantic question)
- How are the feelings expressed? (Communicative question
- How are the feelings evaluated? (Values question)
- What techniques or strategies are available for dealing with emotions? (Management question)

In the area of intercultural mediations, as well, these fundamental questions play a large role for emotional perception and presence: Here it will be of importance to know what points and events in the conflicts lead to which emotional attitudes, and corresponding to which opportunities for action? Thus, these questions can be explained in mediation sessions. Another possibility is for mediators to go into this subject in preliminary explanations

Primary emotions are always connected with what are denoted "bodily arousal," "mental appraisal," and "moral/cultural approval." This means that these feelings are bio-chemically guided, trigger c0gnitive evaluations, and attracted by moral conceptualizations.. In particular, anger can easily find itself transformed to rage, whose goal is the debilitation of the integrity or the safety of the opposing party. To boot, rage can escalate into violence, to coerce practical or symbolic changes and/or crush key social values.

Reaction to problems can be expressed in, for example, revenge, neglect, excuses, violence, passive acceptance, denial, dissimulation, concealment, repetition or the ritual of reconciliation, a handshake, or official exonerations.. Fearfulness, shame, or guilt, however, often stand in the way of reconciliation as instances of control.

These facts are especially relevant for mediators for two reasons. First, knowledge of different forms emotional expression lead to a broadening of competence in the mediation process itself. Second, mediators avoid possible false conclusions through projection of one's own emotional culture upon the vis-à-vis' emotional culture. In the culturally specific part of this book, the subject will be addressed once more, concretely (cf. chap. 5.6.2).

4.6.7 Power and Power Imbalances

Power imbalances constitute a large, structure-related subject that mediators have repeatedly to confront. Bringing balance into the parties' confrontation, and to synchronize their actions are steps that can e helpful go the leveling in power imbalances in mediation. One must see to it that all parties are given approximately the same amount of time for speaking, and that they strive for a process-oriented procedure, from which a symmetrical process can emerge. The latter process must be related to the steps of the negotiations, as well as to the sequences which may perhaps be followed in the discovery of a solution.

- Balances of power can become a burden when one party is "stronger," Frequently, power imbalances emerge in connection with conflicts over labor in which one party to the conflict possesses more power than the other—for example, in disputes between those in charge of work assignments and those assigned to the work, between persons in charge and those

below, Power balances can also be found, however, in situations in which special structures are given, as for example in parent-child or teacher-pupil relationships. In intercultural situations, still other factors play a role, as well, that are less important in intra-cultural ones. Factors that must be responded to unconditionally in intercultural mediations are here given and discussed:
- Gender
- Positions in the social hierarchy arising from profession or employment, age, sex, etc,
- Speech, speech-abilities, and speech barriers
- Minority versus majority cultures—balancing of the weight of social power?
- Cultural background of the mediators

Membership in a given gender group can create inequalities of power. In certain role connections, for instance, it is often men who are to be found in a more powerful position than women. In intercultural mediations, this series of topics, too, is to be considered more pointedly. Every cultural group has its own assessment of gender position, and therefore of defined roles, opportunities, rights, and duties. From a Western viewpoint, it often seems to us that, in other cultures, man and woman have no "equality of rights." The reason why we notice a difference here is that out own, ethnocentric definition of "equality of rights" is an entirely different one from those used. Thus, if the gender-specific role relationship fails to correspond to our criteria of equality in rights, we often observe: "With others, equality of rights for men and women does not prevail." Here it will be in order to conduct an exact review of what role-pretensions, expectations, and motivations underlie a premise or an action, and whether these backgrounds may possibly evoke power imbalances in the view of the conflicting parties.

Naturally, then, positions in social hierarchies often play a role in conflicts as well. So the "boss" usually has more authority than the employees under him, the teacher more than the pupils, and elders more than their children. In intercultural connections, again, these structures of authority receive an altogether special coloration (cf. White 2001).

In many societies, persons have especially great authority if they have reached an advanced age. Or they have authority because they are vessels of "healing powers," because they drive a particular automobile, because they have a special skin color, or belong to a certain clan, distinguished family, or ethnic group.

In Western culture, we can begin with the fact that we have a relatively homogeneous conception of who has authority and who does not, and how important or unimportant it is for someone to be powerful— read: to what extent are persons oriented to the mighty or not, and what influence do these latter have on, for instance, processes of conflict-solution. In intercultural mediations, these questions will play an important role as well, for the question of power and authority is often joined together with certain ways of behavior, and especially with emotions. In intercultural mediation, these questions are worked out in view of the definition of power and of the powerful.

When a great inequality of power or authority breaks out owing to the membership of the conflicting parties in minority or majority cultures, it is often the case that cultural differences shift to the foreground, to compensate for or level out the inequality of power. Here, culture is made use of as an equalization strategy (cf. chap. 4.6.5).

When representatives of both groups sit in a mediation, it can easily happen that the entire socio-historical context is drawn into the mediation. Obviously, this societally relevant power relationships must be addressed the moment that they are introduced into the mediation. Then it is the task of the mediators to determine, with the parties to the conflict, at what locus the societal situation affects the conflict that now must be concretely worked out, and how, then, one is further to proceed. Particularly, a center of gravity may be that the parties to the conflict learn to perceive their respective vis-à-vis as individuals, and not as members of a "collective."

When mediators confront inequalities of empowerment in situations of mediation, it can be helpful to take into consideration that there are differing political concepts of the structure of relations between majorities and minorities. Thus, if two conflicting parties come to the mediation session and introduce their own majority-minority conflict, then it is important that the mediators know the distinct political concepts of majority and minority cultures, and be able to relate them in view of the context of the parties in conflict as well. When this is possible on the part of the mediators, then culturally specific manners of behavior and thinking can be demonstrated, on the one hand, on the other, adjustments of the perspectives of the conflicting parties and the mediators can be introduced regarding the sensibilities prevailing between members of minorities and minorities. Our orientation is that of a model of Flechsig (1998):

Political concept of relations between majority and minority cultures	Description
Assimilation	Complete or extensive adaptation of members of a minority culture and a majority culture.
Segregation	Complete or extensive frontiers between minorities and majority (cultural and perhaps territorial).
Coexistence	Peaceful coexistence between minorities, and majority culture, with minimal contact.
Integration	Incorporation of minority cultures, with maintenance and further development of their cultural identity, and broadening or enrichment of the cultural standard developed by the majority.
Evolution	Development of new, heterogeneous majority cultures, with the introduction of specific strengths of the original majority and minority cultures.

Graph: Political concept of relations between majority and minority cultures

If a power imbalance becomes evident in situations of mediation on grounds of the real situation of majority and minorities in the country, then it is a matter, in terms of the political concepts standing behind this series of problems, of societies in which minorities have been integrated, segregated, or assimilated. The reason for this analysis of the situation is that, with the application of these concepts to societies, members of minorities will tend to feel the dominance of the majority culture over the minority culture. Then the latter culture may at times come to expression in the mediation session as an undercurrent, if not directly. Precisely when the parties fail to introduce this social conflict directly, it is all the more important for the mediators to be informed on the facts of the socio-political relations between majority and minority culture, and to work with those relations.

When the mediators belong to a particular cultural group, they usually speak a particular language, that of one or the other conflicting parties. If they have a particular nationality, it can happen that the cultural background of the mediators sharpens the power imbalance already at hand, above all when neutrality cannot be guaranteed.

As we have already addressed the matter of language, we can here proceed to a sensitive point that is probably is one of the deciding factors in intercultural mediations for a balance of empowerment. Language, fluency in language, and barriers in language can introduce powerful factors into the situation of mediation. It frequently occurs that one party will manifest a substantially weaker knowledge of a language than will the other. Even when the mediators support the linguistically weaker group through repetition or other speech techniques, that party nevertheless usually has the weaker position in the imbalance of power: they can neither express themselves as spontaneously, nor are on the same speech level qualitatively. Further, there then arises a feeling of inferiority in its own linguistic competences, which the in question imbalance scarcely moderates.

Manners of thinking and reacting in the conflict can be better understood through the linguistic approach invoked. In this context, aphorisms, metaphors, tales, and visual images play a special role, clarifying relations in conflicts, possibilities of reaction, and involvement with situations of conflict and their transformation. In addition, maxims, metaphors, and images suggest, imply, and associate profound cultural conceptions, and thereby provide for a glance into the cultural wisdom of groups of human beings. According to Lederach (1996), proverbs are variously interpretable, and thus create manifold /ies for an approach to culturally specific realities, the sense of conflict resident therein, and solutions.

Translators are often brought into mediations. It is true, of course, that, as a rule, this guarantees that the linguistic and verbal aspect of the negotiations be served in a correct and qualitatively valuable manner. There will always remain, however, concepts that, considered culturally, have an altogether distinct coloration, and one that cannot be unconditionally mediated. If translators are introduced only for one party, a further imbalance can quickly appear: the party favored with the translation usually takes up a higher proportion of time, and pauses in the translation may crop up that lead to interruptions in the train of elements in course. This need not always have negative consequences, however. In given instances, these pauses pacify emotionally charged subjects of conversation—"de-escalate them." On occasion, then, pauses in a translation can even bring calm and distance into the process. Negative remarks and observations, which otherwise might quickly provoke a further insult or wound, will not as likely do so with the introduction of translators. Each party has a little time to consider and the spontaneous reaction decelerates. Translators also frequently offer a "filter," through which the message must be sent first, the message acquires the character of a pure piece of "information," without great emotional participation on the part of the sender.

By way of translations, then, it can also occur that the parties will consider once again whether they really wish to send a message or not: each message costs the time of translation, serenity, and patience. Naturally, it is equally likely that the parties will become impatient with the time-embezzling translations, and finally no longer know what to do in the meantime. In a case like this, translation can escalate emotions instead of "bringing them down."

It can easily happen to mediators working with distinct cultural groups or individuals, that they prefer too address the party whose language they themselves speak and understand: familiarity with their own language gives them a higher assurance in their behavior and creates confidence in the party at hand. In such a case neutrality can more easily begin to vacillate than one thinks. Even from the viewpoint of the parties to the conflict, this can present a difficulty: the party who have lived their lives pretty much in the language of the mediators, or even becomes very good in it, can always come into direct contact with the mediators, or has even mastered it, than can the other party, and so attempts to engage the mediation team in ordinary conversation, can always get into direct contact with the mediators more readily than can the other party.

If this direct communication is not consciously formed by way of the mediators, this party can easily attain a communicative overbalance. Correspondingly, observation and perception of cultural and linguistic differences is reinforced.

If the team of mediators and the team of translators work together, then, according to Liebe (1996), communalities in work can be discovered. Then a systematic translation requires a clear structure of communication. When the translation proceeds in this manner, a communication between the parties can be assured. If the mediators are unable to translate, communication between the parties collapses. It must further be clear that the translators are translating for the mediators—who are, after all, in charge of the process—and not only for the parties to the parties to the conflict, bypassing the mediators. When the teams, respectively, of mediators and translators merge in a common "setting," the translators can support the process, and work in the spirit of the mediators.

A solution for intercultural situations of mediation is supposed to consist in a team of mediators being introduced into the process to whom both languages are familiar. This would at least afford a good beginning as far as linguistic neutrality were to be concerned. Then,, however, translators ought still to be introduced into the process who translate the contribution of the one party for the other. Here again a balance would then be produced, and both parties ought to wait for the pauses in the translation, and neither of the two parties would attain to a special dominance in respect of the linguistic imbalance. Furthermore, the conflicting parties can both speak in their own respective languages, and the introduction of the native language would bring their emotions and needs to find expression, in authentic wise, through its respective native language. An "acting" will be possible, which can very authentically convey "how those involved are doing," and, for instance what expectations they have. If, on the contrary, persons speak in a more or less familiar foreign language, frequently emotions and needs are not adequately expressed, and a linguistically conditioned hesitation enters the foreground of the communication.

Language - and competency in language - are, assuredly, factors that can quickly produce balance of power in situations of mediation. It is important, then, to make this point even in the explanations preceding intercultural mediations, I order to find the appropriate path for dealing with them, and to address the matter of balance of balance of "empowerments" in mediation and to be able to "even them out."

4.6.8 Dynamics of Escalation in Situations of Intercultural Conflict

In numerous textbooks on, and introductions to, mediation, mediators are provided with manageable and up-to-date models of typical dynamics of conflictive escalation. For a utilization of these models at a deeper level, as well as for their potential complementation, we should here like to call particular attention to the model proposed by Glasl (1997, 2000). Among the typical factors that may emerge in contexts of intercultural mediation, let us now focus on three specific elements that especially stimulate the dynamics of escalation in situations of intercultural conflict.\

According to Haumersen and Liebe (20001), escalation in situations of intercultural conflict is attended by special dynamisms. Three determinative levels, closely bonded, or knotted together, come front and center here: the levels of a psychological strategy of communication, a political ideology, and an orientation to behavior. We should like to present these three levels here, briefly, as Haumersen and

Liebe express them, since they are of importance for the management of this subject and its application in practice.

The level of the <u>psychological strategy of communication</u> implies that culture is one variable among many that play a role in intercultural conflict. The individual is marked by the process of socialization, as well as by the process of enculturation. In other words, besides the cultural factor, and the inherited collective cultural identity of the cultural community, human beings are also marked by a personal identity factor. It is often difficult to distinguish, from without, which elements of personality are shaped by the cultural and which by the personal. On the one hand, the cultural limits observed between two parties can lead to there being objective obstacles that preclude further common action. On the other hand, it may also occur that cultural differences are stressed in order to win strategic advantages in the upcoming or ongoing communication. Thus, one could speak of the cultural factor being utilized with the purpose of achieving one's own advantages, or to counter possible imbalances (cf. chap. 4.6.5). Should this phenomenon enter the picture, and should the other party perceive that culture is being introduced as a tool and a strategy, then the dynamics of escalation may shoot for the sky.

As for the second level, which Haumersen and Liebe (1999) denote the <u>level of political ideology,</u> the premise is that, in every person, prejudices against other persons lurk, and that these may to some extent be transformed into stereotypes. Indeed, besides these prejudices, everyone entertains an inner predilection for his or her own social identity and culture as being of greater value than others. This attitude is called the <u>ethno-centrist attitude.</u> In intercultural conflicts, it can easily occur that, when, on the basis of cultural differences, persons fail to be able to understand one another, or to make themselves understood, then their reference to their own culture is reinforced, and they apply their own models of cultural interpretation and perception all the more earnestly. After all, these models offer behavioral security. Precisely when this is the case, conflicts escalate all the more rapidly, since, frequently, one's own self-reflection is now deprived of reliability. What goes missing is a view of the situation as a whole, and, and stereotypical enunciations and manifestations now displace the adoption of a personal relationship with one's neighbor. Individuals are transformed into representatives of the collective. The original object of conflict is now fraught with the dimension of some political ideology or other. When this is the case, stereotypes and prejudices must be resolutely addressed, in order to develop them in the dialogue, and to give them more attention. Now one's own values become visible, and a new appraisal of judgmental criteria can supervene.

As the third moment of escalation in intercultural conflict, we must cite <u>behavioral orientation</u>. The latter implies that, in intercultural situations, behavioral insecurities arise. Parties are incapable of forming an estimate of their neighbor's reactions or modes of behavior and activity. This can lead to ways of acting that occasion the impairment of communication and the escalation of the conflict. Only the presence of a third party can work de-escalating, since now the attention of both parties is automatically diverted.

4.7 Cultural Orientation and its Consequences

If - as described above (chap.2.1) - we understand, under cultural orientation, that pattern of perception and activity constructed, and repeatedly altered, by individual members or groups of a given culture, then it is indispensable for intercultural mediators that they know, and deal with, the variances in the bases of individual cultural orientations.

Thus, we should like to make a comparative presentation of certain relevant cultural orientations (according to Flechsig 2001) that work as settings in intercultural contexts.

Settings for the natural, cultural, and social environment can be *grosso modo* distinguished in three categories:

- Control of environments
- Wish for harmony with environments
- Conceptualization of dependency on environments

If we consider the context of mediation, these conceptions can mean that the social process of intercultural mediation is seen as open to being controlled—that, in mediation, one either evaluates interpersonal harmony as worthy of pursuit, or else withdraws and leaves control in the mediation process to other participants.

Conceptualizations regarding time are extremely diverse. Persons have either a "uni-dimensional" or a "pluri-dimensional" understanding of time. The first group of persons concentrates on a task at a particular time, with concrete temporal presuppositions. For the mediation process, this conceptualization has the meaning that beginning, process, and end of mediation situations are exactly determined with respect to time frame. A person who thinks pluri-dimensionally would possibly be irritated at this, and would become impatient, as s/he would prefer to develop several tasks and problems simultaneously, and that their social relationships are more important than observance of durations and times.

Conceptualizations of time are especially conspicuous in mediations that are to be described with fixity of temporal units or with the broad flow of time. When someone has a notion of slow, fluctuating time, or indeed the concept that time moves now more slowly, now at a greater speed, then it is rather to be expected that this person would emphasize the secondary importance of schedule. Interruptions are regarded as normal; sessions begin when everyone is there. Such a conception often goes against the grain of those who earnestly want to begin at the time agreed upon, and to proceed in the mediation point by point. "Time is money." It is the duty of the mediator to point out these highly conflict-laden conceptions, and in a given case to mediate them lest any new "time" problems arise.

Finally, we must point out that there are somewhat strange-seeming concepts of time, for Western-oriented persons that allow other persons to see all actions, decisions, and events under the aspect of the past. Basically, those who have this notion of time constantly prefer an examination of compatibility, as to whether plans, agreements, prognoses, etc., are in agreement with their life history, their group traditions, and their cultural history. Obviously it is not easy to mediate this concept with others, who are oriented rather to the present or the future. As we know, the goal of mediation is to make a satisfactory future "win-win" situation possible for all parties.

When differing attitudes toward action are taken into consideration, what dominate here are two diametrically opposed forms of action. In many cultures, active action, achievement, and the attainment of a goal are thought of as worth striving for, and they contribute to the satisfaction of the individual. In other cultures, orientations are preferred that emphasize the moment, and professional and personal satisfaction in contemplation and meditation, in speaking and keeping silent - in brief, in existing. For mediation, this means that persons who prefer an active lifestyle more likely bring themselves actively into the situation, and run the risk of dominating the situation of mediation. Persons more passive or being-oriented lay their center of gravity first and foremost on the observation of the situation, and are inclined to conduct themselves hesitantly. Then the duty of the mediators is to attempt to reverse a possible imbalance, and purposefully to intervene.

A considerable spectrum divides persons' conduct in the area of communication.

"High context" communication (Hall 1990) is always to be found where as considerable quantity of information is collected concerning the partners to the conversation before there is a chance to think of making decisions or undertaking to catalyze agreements. This information flows not only by way of verbal enunciation to common friends,, status, or earlier encounters, but frequently by way of nonverbal semantics, as well, such as tone of voice, body language, facial expression, and eye contact.

By contrast, in contexts of "low context" communication, context-related information concerning personal relations is less needed for the purpose of reaching valid and binding agreements. Rather, the determining element is whether all factually relevant content be enunciation in words, or be composed in writing.

Related to situations of intercultural mediation is the task of taking into account the fact that "high context" persons prefer to solve conflicts personally, if at all possible, that is, with little reference to the actual matter. The mediation process is accompanied by poetry, proverbs, and linguistic excursus. Simultaneously, one prefers to renounce rigid sets of rules: none such is required in the matter at hand, if familiarity and trust has already been built up, and prevails, between the persons. On the other hand, "low context" persons prefer to conduct direct communication, and to depersonalize a conflict.

Similarly situated are the preferences in the spectrum of communication from direct to indirect exchange. When speakers prefer the direct style of communication, many conflicts are discussed face to face. Here, as a rule, mediators or "go-betweens" are not called upon.

"Open" criticism is evaluated positively, while a behavior of indirect communication is regarded as problematic, or even "mendacious." However, when the cultural orientation of indirect communication prevails, conflicts are worked out according to tested methods, by recognized mediators or "go-betweens." The triangulation of conflicts, furthermore, and indirect forms of communication serve to avoid a loss of face with the parties at odds. In intercultural mediation, much care must be taken that neither side suffers such a loss of face, since otherwise the entire process will be damaged or broken off. Thus, when strongly diverging styles of communication are in question, it is of fundamental importance to bring to light the various characteristics and effects of style, and of these styles.

An astonishing variation in expression resides in the poles of communication of "expressive and instrumental" styles. When participants in communication prefer an expressive style, they express their emotions in gestures and body language. In mediation situations, at times, this kind of communication has rather imprecise effects. At these times, in a suitable manner, mediators must make it "communicable," especially when the other party to the conflict prefers instrumental styles of communication instead. In this case, everything will be staked on factuality, pragmatics, and goal-directedness. Emotions seem to the subjects of instrumental styles as somewhat unprofessional, and frequently not serviceable for the matter at hand. Whether these distinctions in the exercise of expressive and instrumental styles are interfering with the mediation process will have to be made clear, of course, on the basis of participants' reactions.

Finally, let us cite the use of formal and informal channels of communication. Persons who communicate formally like to emphasize business and social etiquette. If formal forms of communication are announced, what then occurs is, for instance, that persons with a higher rank or higher position in the hierarchy will be accorded corresponding respect, both when they speak, and in the formulation of the mediation process. Persons with a cultural orientation who prefer informal communication consider progress more important than maintenance of antique structures or usages. With them, one can relax, and calmly chat. They do feel uneasy, though, if they notice that, on the other side, formalisms reign, and social rank entails a preferential treatment. In a situation of mediation, they see the establishment of personal relations rather as superfluous; they are principally concerned with work on the conflict, and with reaching the goal of the mediation.

Finally, variant cultural orientations are very clearly reflected in the distinction between private and public space. Accordingly, there are very different needs with respect to:

- Personal space-requirements
- Preferred "body distance"
- The physical space recognized as private or public
- The rules of behavior acknowledged in the spheres of the private and of the public

For intercultural mediation, these culturally varying spatial orientations imply the attention that must be paid to the kind of spatial boundaries, in which the mediation is to be conducted, must be observed. Just as important is the observance of "body distance" between mediator and conflicting parties. This question is still further differentiated in terms of the imperatives of gender-specific relationships. Roughly stated, it is Western culture at work when it is assumed that the private sphere enjoys an extensive boundary, and generally includes the family and close friends. Other cultures know no concept of "private"— for them, what is crucial is the attitude of lesser or greater "publicness." What we call the "private," or even the "intimate," plays out only between two persons in the protected space. Further, by many cultures the situation of mediation is regarded as private and confidential, but as more or less a public process, in which rules are to be observed that are appropriate to such a context. But that does not mean that just anyone may take part in the mediation; still, it is altogether possible that other, affiliated persons may be invited.

Let us now turn to a cultural orientation that not only plays an exceptional role with respect to cultural dimension (cf. Hofstede, our chap. 5.1), but also has its place in intra- as well as intercultural mediation techniques. Attitudes toward power, authority, determine the measure in which the less powerful individuals or groups of a culture expect and accept that power is distributed equally or unequally. When members of cultures are more hierarchically oriented, it can depend on hierarchies of age, gender, and origin, and frequently also hierarchies of occupation, which appraise mental work as of a higher value than manual work. Persons with this attitude often have an interest in getting respect in the conversational situation with their title or status. However, this strategy frequently fails to win out when the other party to the conflict takes a different attitude toward authority: by contrast with hierarchical orientations, egalitarian attitudes may be noticed, that do not hold status, titles, and formal positions as especially meaningful for the success of the mediation process. Instead, their point of departure is that the conflicting parties and the mediator are of equal worth, and ought to represent no unequal power structures, not to mention any acceptance of them. It is obvious that mediators in intercultural contexts will have to place a special accent on the transparency of these "visible" attitudes toward authority, with their implications of expectation and approach, unless they wish to risk the mediation concerns going down in defeat.

Cultures and societies are essentially different in their orientations to individualist or collectivist outlines. In collectivist orientations, the interests of individuals are unequivocally subordinated to those of the community. Group solidity protects the members and gives them comfort and assurance, while the group receives fidelity and obedience in the other direction. "We" takes precedence over "I." When someone enunciates the supposed opinion of the majority, this is seen as a sign of loyalty. Power and authority are exercised by opinion controllers, who represent the goals of the community in a special manner.

By contrast, the main characteristics of individual orientations are to seen in connections that are less tight, and "I" precedes "we." Personal identity is a goal worth striving for. Law and the administration of justice are equal for every citizen. To be able to say "I," and to hold dissenting opinions, are signs of cultural standards in which the "I" is accepted.

In mediation, the effect of these orientations is extremely differentiated. Thus, it can occur that an individual with a collectivist orientation does not participate in the mediation process, but, in order to be sure of the necessary "backing," only emerges with other representatives of his or her relational group. Nevertheless, we may not speak of an intercultural group mediation here: the "we" of this relational group corresponds not to the choir of a plurality of individuals, but only to a single voice. In certain circumstances, a party with an individualistic orientation may feel outnumbered by a collectivist-minded party of this kind. In this case, it would be the task of the mediator to render the meaning of the group for the collectivist-oriented party to the conflict transparent, and thereby to dismantle the fears.

Individuals and groups may represent relevant attitudes, for the mediation, that must be indicated as universalistic or particularistic. The approach to intercultural mediation that we propose endeavors to underscore the universalistic course of the "generic culture" (cf. chap. 2.1) as the fundament of any mediation. Still, following the example of Western-African interaction, we seek also to demonstrate its special particularistic stamp. After all, universalistic orientations stress the application of universally valid rules, strategies, and methods. Agents of particularistic orientations, on the other hand, incline to emphasize their uniqueness and differentiation. With these, the valid elements are the special cultural elements of the individual group and their social networks to the extent that valid worldwide claims are not adapted or subordinated. We often meet this phenomenon in a locus in which there is question of, for example, the recognition of general human rights in Asian or African cultural space. In relation to intercultural mediation, this state of affairs can catalyze the eruption of implicit lines of conflict that lurk in content. In certain cultures, freedom of the individual is understood and reconstructed in extremely controvertible ways. Competition signs the attitudes that respect breadth, size, and speed, emphasize goods, money, and materiality, and value ambition, achievement, and pleasure in making decisions. By contrast, material success has less effect on motives of persons of a cooperative outlook. If we address the diametrically opposed orientations of activity, we distinguish the competition-oriented modality and the cooperation-oriented modality. Quality of life, and the act of assistance, or of cooperation, are esteemed. How do both cultural orientations work ojt in respective situations or "settings"? Competition-oriented persons often embody "hard" positions, and, if they insist on them, they can become stubborn, and the representatives of a cooperative answer feel "made fun of," since their "soft" positions are not satisfactorily respected. If these controversial orientations are conditioned not personally, but culturally, then the mediator must "work out" the subject with the conflicting parties; and, if need be, s/he must take measures to avoid a looming imbalance. Positively, these diverse orientations can work in favor of a reconciliation by mediation. The party with the competition-oriented temperaments will admit satisfaction, if a solution is worked out with material result, attainment of a goal, or acknowledgement of an achievement. The other party to the conflict, the one with the basically cooperative attitude, will probably be pleased with the reconciliation, as it assures a comfortable and agreeable atmosphere.

In a case of high intra-cultural or intercultural variation, one finds orientation to order and structure. Highly structured orientations here imply that ambiguities and equivocations will be inhibited as far as possible. Predictability and calculable conflicts are preferred to blind situations and other uncertainties, clear hierarchies and delineations of competency are respected, and with all of the inevitable demands, stress readily supervenes. Everything is seen as depending on avoiding uncertainties (cf. chap. 5.1). How different the attitude of the subjects of flexible orientations! They, instead, are ready for risk, and tolerant in their dealings with situations and persons. They are altogether accepting of deviations from rules or from opinions. For them, conflicts are part of the self-evident in human coexistence. For mediation, the process and the content, these brief orientations have considerable effect. Lofty expectations require of the mediator a presentation of clear rules, while even here small deviations can lead to irritation. In mediations, bones of contention are, as a rule, difficult to calculate in advance. Thus, persons of high-structured orientations put themselves under considerable pressure to consign agreements, and the outcome of agreements, to paper with precision, and to insist on strict adherence to the. Otherwise, they fear, mistrust between the parties and the mediator may appear on the scene. Persons of a flexible attitude toward order and structure see things differently. They can live with it when deviations appear in the mediation process and its course, or an agreement is adhered to, granted, not literally, in its meaning. Rules are supposed to serve the conflicting parties to in coming to an conclusion, and therefore are changeable. It would be uncomfortable for a person with flexible orientations to have to think that all participants in the mediation would be subjected to "stiff" rules. Clearly, it will not be easy for mediators in intercultural contexts to work out precisely these very heterogeneous cultural patterns of attitude. After all, in Western contexts, mediation easily proceeds in high structures, not to mention with an orientation to rules and sealed with written agreements after the conclusion of the solution phase.

It is culturally divergent styles of thinking that supply the background for declarations and argumentations. Here we distinguish cognitive figures who see things either inductively or deductively. With inductively thinking persons, the point of departure for their thinking is the assortment of individual data, concrete connections, and verifiable experiences. The development of models and hypotheses is grounded on observation and experimentation. For situations of intercultural mediation, this cultural orientation is of importance. Its starting point consists of demonstrable facts and statistics, little accompanied by emotions. As we have shown in the SMART model (chap. 3.3), this model enjoys is particularly preferred in meditations in the Western context. An objection would be that numerous persons with deductive ways of thinking start with grand theories—drawn from daily life or scientific—and draw their conclusions from these. This manner of cultural orientations can occasionally be stated in slogans to the effect that inductive styles of thought correspond to a scientifically qualified worldview, while deductive styles see themselves find themselves indebted, instead, to a mental-spiritual image of the human being, and an "ideological" understanding of the world. For intercultural mediation, the course of a confrontation between these antagonistic orientations culminates in a challenge that which mediators are extremely hard put to reconcile or influence. After all, we are dealing with cognitive construct been developed by one party or the other for the purpose of an interpretation of life, and have found it tried and true for this end. To be sure, it is certainly important that mediators see that no harm be done when one party makes fun of the thought style of the other because this style has no place in their system of coordinates.

More critical, perhaps, for intercultural mediation is the opposition between linear and holistic thought styles. When one culture is attached to linear styles of thinking, it prefers the dissection and compartmentalization of events and concepts into cause-effect chains, means-end chains, or logical chains. One proceeds analytically. On the other hand, persons from cultures that prefer a holistic manner of thought think in a different way. Here, thinking and working are integrated. "Synthetic manners of proceeding are preferred.

When persons of such divergent ways or thinking encounter in mediation, they become irritated. Holistically inclined persons like to speak in metaphors, idioms, and analogies, and thereby to express themselves in conflicts in a way corresponding to the elements of their thinking. By contrast, analytically, or "linearly" thinking persons prefer to express themselves pragmatically. Events, subjects, and activities are "operationalized" - thus, divided into small units. It is a task of the mediator to accept this style of thinking as of equal dignity and adequacy. They must try to see to it that the parties respect each other's different cultural orientations.

In the cultural sciences, especially in that of cultural psychology, expressions of causal attribution play a role in culturally diverse contexts. We receive information concerning the causes persons adduce to explain certain occurrences: cultural variants are principally related to the three orientations, namely, "personal achievement," "coincidence," and "fate":

1. Persons think that they can reach their goals, and change the world, by their own capabilities and achievement.
2. Persons think that failures and successes are to be attributed to unforeseeable external circumstances.
3. Persons assume that the course of events is predestined.

For mediation: Especially in the respective phases of the presentation and elucidation of the conflict, these seemingly incommensurable attitudes have considerable consequences. In the presentation of the points of conflict, persons whose attribution of clear thinking and successful outcome is to their own powers will stress their own contributions and abilities as advancing or having advanced the conflict in question. They think positively, because they value their own contribution highly. The basic premise of persons who make coincidence responsible for events, is that risks cannot be calculated, and thus that any activities, being senseless, might as well be omitted. Persons, who, instead, take predestination as the key to their attributions, make astral constellations, or what is theologically foreordained, or mystically determined imperatives responsible for the course of events.

When these three philosophical constructs meet in mediation, it is no simple matter for the mediator to guide the mediation process to its final phase. Persons who attribute success to achievement can be expected to make active and engaged contributions in mediation which will advance the process and problem solution. Persons whose causal attribution is to coincidence give scant occasion for the assumption that they will work towards a successful solution. After all, they see even their own activities as determined by "happenstance," so that they assign them little value. Finally, persons who rely on predestination can expected, in mediation, to see all of their activities as serving their foreordained lives, no matter who or what may intervene in them along the way: observed from without, their operation seems passive, but in the inner sight of these persons, is the active fulfilment of their destiny.

We here compose a table of basic intercultural orientations and standards, which are of practical relevance:

Cultural Orientations (as in Flechsig 2001)	Abbreviated description
Attitudes toward the environment	• Control • Desire for harmony • Conceptualizations of dependency
Attitudes toward time	• Concentration • Constant and moving • Orientation to past, present, and future
Action	• Active/passive • Being and doing
Communication	• High context / low context • Direct/indirect • Expressive/instrumental
Space	• Private/public
Authority and power	• Equality • Hierarchy • Inequality
Style of thought	• Inductive/deductive
Causal attribution	• Own attainment / coincidence / destiny
Collectivistic/individualistic	• Collectivistic/individualistic • Universalistic/particularistic
Competition	• Competition oriented / cooperative
Structure	• High degree of structure / flexibility

Graph: Cultural Orientations

4.8 Intercultural Influences in the Setting of Mediation

1. If a mediation is requested or demanded, the primary question is that of the most suitable place to meet. Suitability is determined primarily according to the comfort of the conflicting parties. Often a neutral place is recommended, i.e. a place acceptable to both parties in the same way. In urgent cases, the place is voted on (chosen by a vote), especially when a suitable mediator is present and can lead the mediation in an authentic manner. It is altogether possible for the conflict to be arbitrated in the house or office of a person of high social rank: in numerous cultures, it is the duty of a person of a certain status to be concerned in this way for her/his entrusted "clients."

2. When the mediation is conducted in the context of Western cultures, it is generally expected that a structure will be encountered, supported by official "formality," and guaranteed by the parties' assurance of their own roles. Other cultures, to the contrary encourage informal and not very rigid structures in mediation. Here the opportunities for social interaction are front and center (cf. 4.7).

3. When what is at issue is the selection of a mediator in an intercultural context, qualified persons apply for the position of moderator or assistant, where it is actually the parties themselves who solve their problem. Here, age can play a less important role in the selection. On the other hand, if the conflicting parties have a more sophisticated experience in the field of the conflict, the mediator's age works as a key to the confidence of the conflicting parties. In many cultures, it is all but expected of the wise older men or women who have the role of mediator—just as it is in religion, politics, and the economic system—come forward as persons with leadership qualities, persons who will actively guide the process. One characteristic of the suitability of mediators in intercultural mediation seems indisputably to be neutrality toward the parties, matched by just as deep a respect for these parties.

4. The mediation process itself may be influenced by very much differing factors. Many conflicting parties are interested in the background of their cultural socialization are interested in attacking problems promptly and impartially and realistically. They may possibly confront a party that first needs to strike a personal relationship in order to address the problem. Or again, other parties to the conflict on a successive development of points of conflict, and are slightly irritated when another party would like to take up several problems at a time (cf. chap. 4.7). Just as powerfully, various conceptions bubble up in the mediation process when it is the form of arguing and speaking that is at issue. Thus, heated argumentation may affect the one party in a disturbing manner, since, for them, it hinders listening, and finding a solution; while members of other cultures see heated argument as an expression of the importance of a problem, and of the degree of a person's engagement. The conversation becomes a drama, and narratives are recounted that, for otherwise inclined persons, do not belong to the subject. There are gesticulations, at times even cries and roars. What for members of the one side is self-evident, for those of the other may be sheerly accessory, and thus superfluous: for the latter, speaking in the mediation means permitting to inform, to discuss, to address, and to allow others to do the same. How mediators can react to such diverse forms of expression, cannot be set in a rule. Instead, it is important to intervene promptly when these forms of expression begin to deteriorate, and no longer to further the intercultural process of mediation.

5. As for the role of the individual in intercultural mediation, we must distinguish two paradigmatic orientations: the individualistic, and the collectivistic (cf. chap 5,1). It would scarcely be sensible to challenge the parties to speak in the first person, if it is known that one party has a collectivist attitude, and assigns the grammatical first person the meaning of the collectivistic first person.

6. Much has been written, and much discussion conducted, concerning the series of problems constituting, and consequent upon, loss of face in the conflict. For intercultural mediation, therefore, special caution is in order: the parties' face is to be guaranteed at all cost. Many parties assign a high value to the form of excuse that contributes to the solution of the conflict. It is not embarrassing, shameful, or painful to them if, by innuendo, or even openly, they are accused of "being wrong." It is only required that the other side acknowledge the sincerity of the excuse or apology, and acknowledges it with a formula of forgiveness. Not to be underestimated is the phenomenon appearing in Old-Asian or African situations: certain conflicts ought not, if possible, to be named and acknowledged through direct communication. Instead, a go-between is needed, to take charge of the conflict in tried and true fashion. For conflicting parties of other cultural orientations, however, it is all the more "painful" to solve a conflict through third persons,, because of the opinion that it can be solved without this.

7. When it is emotions that are at issue, and these frequently appear in conflicts, cultures have differing responses and evaluations when it comes to the expression of feelings. One party may perhaps not show feelings, because this is supposed to evince strong self-control; it may be simply that objectivity is claimed here, and this group's particular position simply be declared to be the "right one. As with "arguing," above, it is precisely important that the other party express feelings, in order to demonstrate interest and commitment. Now let us once more address the importance of both cultures being given the opportunity to introduce their orientations.

8. Let us come to the subject of conflict in intercultural mediations, and striving for a goal there. In many mediations, the establishment of whether a party is "right" or "wrong" is to be avoided if at all possible, lest a "chasm" between the two parties begin to yawn. Instead, the point will be to strive for a solution of the conflict on the basis of in rules, and therefore consciously to leave out any appraisals of guilt. Solutions are

attained by give-and-take, so that both parties receive a feeling of justice and equilibrium. How else does it go for culturally differently oriented parties, with whom an understanding of guilt is absorbed as the basis for a solution. We need only cast a brief glance at how, in most regional cultures, however varied their orientations to outcome, in order to be struck that, in most intercultural mediations, the restoration of relations seems to take first place. Then follows the expectation of working together again. In extra-European contexts of cultural mediations, what is at issue is often the acknowledgment of social positions, or of the public demonstration of respectful attitudes. It is true that persons of a Western orientation entertain a different view. For them, the core of the issue is probably rather to ground more profound needs, and to create the possibility of their satisfaction.

9. Now let us consider some essential cultural semantics, semantics that may have an effect in intercultural mediation. In respect of cultural semantics, let us give some culturally specific possibilities of interpretation, as they present themselves in one culture or another.

Gesture?
- Nodding means: no.
- Nodding means: attention.
- Nodding means: yes.
- Nodding means: disinterest.

Mimicry?
- Eye contact: means attention and respect.
- Eye contact: means challenge and disrespectfulness.
- Eye contact: means the establishment of a personal relationship.
- Sneering: shows empathetic sympathy
- Sneering: indicates an attitude of inner aversion.

Laughing?
- Laughing means anger.
- Laughing shows insecurity.
- Laughing means contributing to decorum.
- Laughing shows tension.
- Laughing is a sign of being happy.

Silence?
- Silence is wisdom.
- Silence is grief.
- Silence is politeness
- Silence is agreement.
- Silence is rejection
- Silence is being unsuspecting

Questions?
- Show interest, participation, and attention.
- Are a form of assault.
- Show ignorance.
- Indicate lack of preparation and information.

Threats?
- Show an intent subsequently to injure.
- Are a vent for anger and aggression.
- Are especially introduced as a strategic element.
- Are always prohibited in subsequent activities

Guilt?
- Silence means guilt.
- Loud defence means guilt.
- The silent one is the perpetrator.
- Silence means something to hide.

Excuse?
- Excuse means regret.
- Excuse means acceptance of guilt.
- Excuse means denial of responsibility.
- Excuse means acceptance of guilt.
- Excuse is a strategic measure for the securing of peace.

These few examples are intended as a summary demonstration of the variety of interpretation in intercultural contexts. It is true that there are also contextual and personal variants of interpretation, expression, intent, and perception. However, these are worth another insertion in intercultural connections.

Having now given an introductory survey of subjects and themes of intercultural mediation, we wish to verify them individually, inasmuch as the areas addressed in our regional example deal with Southern Africa. In the culturally specific chapter, we are especially interested in observing compatibilities or incompatibilities between the great regional cultures of the Western world and those of Africa.

5. Mediating Interaction between Westerners and Africans

As mentioned in the chapter on Culture and Interculturalism (see Chapter 2.1), the cultural scientist Hofstede views culture as a dynamic result of programming processes in mental software. This mental software is particularly characterized by the so-called **cultural dimensions** developed by Hofstede. Hofstede's universal approach is relevant to our understanding of mediating interaction between Westerners and Africans because they are based on detectable and widely recognized research results. Although these results paint a picture of cultures based on a set of inter-subjective instruments, the specific cultural profiles are delineated by the people representing the various cultures themselves.

5.1 Introduction to Cultural Dimensions of Southern Africa

We shall now examine the **cultural paradigms** in intercultural mediation described in the preceding Chapter 4.7 in the context of **cultural dimensions** with a special focus on specific characteristics in Southern Africa. One remarkable point is that cultural paradigms related to "power" and "individualistic/collective" are also cultural dimensions. These commonalities are mainly due to the different, generally recognized approaches in cultural sciences. Even so, these commonalities—although they are not identical in meaning and content—are an indication that these terms are especially important for an intimate understanding of a culture in a regional cultural comparison.

Now, we shall briefly review these cultural dimensions, and apply them to the specific cultural context of Southern Africa.

Power distance is defined as the degree "to which the less powerful members of institutions and/or organizations in a country expect or accept that power is distributed unevenly."(Hofstede 1997)

I. **Individualism/collectivism**: This dimension has been a frequent topic of discussion by sociologists, psychologists and anthropologists (Bond 1988 & 1998, Hofstede 1985 & 1997, Kim et al 1994, Kluckhohn & Stroedbeck 1961, Mead 1968, Matsumoto et al 1997, Triandis 1995). Collectively oriented cultures are cultures which have a tendency to enter into social dependencies, which hold bonds between individuals in a community in high esteem and which see themselves as a part of collectives such as a family, employees, ethnic groups or country. They are usually motivated by norms, obligations and values of the community, where communal goals come before personal ones.

In individualistically oriented cultures, individuals generally consider themselves independent and feel only loose ties with the community. Individuals in such cultures are usually motivated by personal preferences, rights and contracts with others. Personal goals come first and foremost and the advantages and disadvantages for the individual are analyzed rationally (Triandis 1995).

II. **Masculinity/femininity**: In so-called masculine societies, gender roles are clearly delineated from one another. Men tend to be decisive with a hard and material orientation, while women strive to be modest, sensitive and interested in the quality of life. In more feminine societies, gender roles overlap. The socialization norms in such societies provide that both men and women be modest and sensitive in the same way and pursue better quality of life in the same way (Hofstede 1997).

III. **Avoiding uncertainty** can be defined as "(...) the degree to which the members of a culture feel threatened by uncertain or unknown situations."(Hofstede 1997)

Hofstede (1997) determined that people in countries in Eastern Africa (in this case: Ethiopia, Kenya, Tanzania, Zambia) are both collectively oriented and display a high **power distance**—the index value was 64 of

100 possible points. As for **masculinity/femininity**, Eastern Africa is mid-range with a total of 41 points, making it a rather **feminine** oriented region with a high **power distance**. With a total of 52 points, the **uncertainty avoidance** index is rather weak for Eastern Africa, i.e. people there have a strong sense of security and are relatively less threatened by unknown situations. At the same time, Hofstede finds that the **individualism** index is relatively low at 27 points, meaning that people there presumably prefer a close-knit collective network and expect their relatives or other "in-group" members to care for them in exchange for their loyalty (Teunissen 1993).

The following is a country-related, trans-cultural comparison of cultural dimensions between a Western and Eastern African country (Germany and Tanzania):

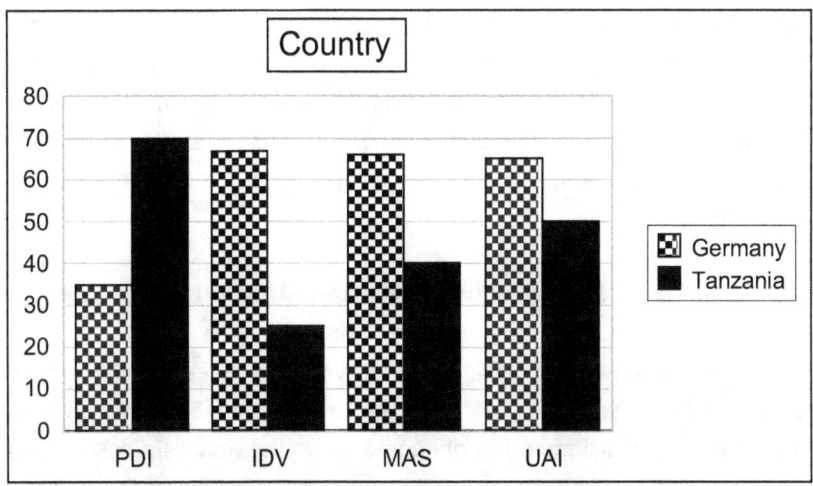

Graph: Germany and Tanzania

This chart shows that the indices for Eastern Africa from the Hofstede study are nearly the same as the values determined for Tanzania from the Teunissen study (1993). One possible explanation for this is that the respondents in the Tanzania study were nearly all involved in development work while the Hofstede study queried people from a private businesses environment. Despite that, the differences for the purpose of cultural dimensions are so small that we can establish a working **hypothesis** for mediation in sub—Saharan cultural contexts:

The probability of encountering conflict in Eastern Africa is high in interactions involving, in particular, the cultural dimensions "high power distance," "very low individualism," "primarily feminine communication structures" and, finally, a lower "need for security". Furthermore, one can assume that, *mutatis mutandis*, the results obtained in numerous countries in Eastern Africa can be applied to countries in **Southern Africa**. This assumption is based on the fact that 70-90% of the people living in countries in greater sub-Saharan Africa are or Bantu origin. Although economic and social developments along with disparities between the countries vary greatly, these disparities can be considered secondary in view of the fact that sets of values and attitudes are important variables in determining people's actions and that these variables only change very slowly from generation to generation. Even so, disparity factors, such as the "nation building" seen in the rainbow society of South Africa, definitely play a major role in intercultural interactions.

5.2 Conflictive Constellations in Western-African Interactions

When people from Western and African contexts meet, conflict can be expected in particular when attitudes and orientations diverge with regard to power distance, the phenomenon of individualism/collectivism and the degree of masculine or feminine organization in the society. Therefore, we now turn to the presentation of essential comparisons and contrasts of specific cultural constellations to identify relevant factors in intercultural disputes. Once again, the emphasis is on constellations at the level of cultural dimensions which are likely to occur in Western-African interaction. Of course, every conflict must be reviewed individually to determine whether and to what extent the features described below apply.

Power distance seems to be a major factor in Southern Africa and is manifested in
- a higher level of need dependencies
- a hierarchy of inequality in which everyone takes his or her legitimate place. This orientation applies to the individual and to the greater family, clans and entire ethnic groups
- a hierarchical order as a expression of existentially approved inequality
- the idea that rulers/authorities are entitled to have privileges and status symbols
- the expectation on the part of subordinates that they will be told what to do and that they will be closely directed as followers
- the concept that the person in charge will act as a generous and caring father
- privileges which dictate that higher birth legitimates succession of rule through *lineage* (the chieftain principle)

In contrast, the low power distance index common in Western countries means
- people take their personal and professional interests into their own hands without necessarily referring to any authorities
- equality of chances and equality of access to the resources of the culture are essential as a basic principle
- power issues are settled by means of a legitimizing discourse and legitimization crises among those in power require dynamic corrections to the system
- the dependency of employees on their superiors in economic enterprises is limited
- there is relatively little emotional distance to those in power

- hierarchies are either deconstructed or closely scrutinized, in favor of generally flatter structures
- subordinates generally make their own decisions in their area of work and only consult higher management levels if it seems absolutely necessary
- the successful formation of teams is mainly more democratic and horizontal rather than hierarchical and vertical
- privileges are viewed more critically and are less respected
- people in charge are recognized more for their performance and function rather than legitimizing their position of power through their attributes or birth right.

The low degree of **Individualism** in Southern Africa is a clear indication of a collectivist culture (see Chapter 4.7) with such features as

- a high degree of identification with *in-groups*, such as family, school, peer groups, neighborhoods and clans
- collective group interests which influence and limit the interests of individuals
- people forming their opinions around the dominant group opinion
- a strong sense of obligation to the *in-group*, especially the family
- a great desire to avoid losing face
- an emotionally warm network of relationships taking precedence over individual self-realization
- orders of rank set according loyalty and the seniority principle rather than market conditions
- harmony and consensus as the ultimate goals of society
- a preference for uniformity ideologies rather than the idea of individual liberties
- a different set of applicable and accepted rights and laws, depending on the group
- an economy based on collective interests

- a critical stance vis-à-vis economic theories imported from the West, since these theories are based on the profit of individuals rather than collective interests
- state influence or censorship of the press
- acceptance of the dominant role of the state in the economic system
- per capita GNP of less than € 2500 per year.

In contrast, Western culture emphasizes **individualism** with
- the autonomy of individuals taking precedence over collective interests
- the anchoring of the right to a private sphere both legally and socially
- every person entitled to voice their own opinion
- laws and rights applicable to each individual person in the same way
- strong political powers to buffer state intervention in economic matters
- political power exercise by voters
- a generally free press—referred to as the "fourth power"
- Western economic theories and entrepreneurial activities focused on individual profit making
- a active role for ideologies of personal liberty and self-realization
- per capita GNP of more than € 2500 per year in nearly all private households (for Germany).

N.B.: The terms for **feminine** or **masculine character** do not refer to specific gender or role characteristics in this context. They are part of a cultural scientific vocabulary for certain orientations and patterns of behavior. They apply in general, regardless of whether a man or woman displays the characteristic.

Although Southern Africa displays a more **feminine** character in contrast to the clearly masculine oriented West, this feature is not very distinct. Even so, the following feminine characteristics can be observed in Southern Africa:

- Human—as opposed to objective—relationships and concern for fellow human beings are fundamental.
- Maintaining values is of primary importance.
- Mutual dependencies and consensual wishes are prevalent.
- People go to work in order to survive.
- People sympathize with those who are less fortunate in life.
- A person's success leads to resentment, people are expected to behave more modestly.
- Intuition plays a big role in making decisions.
- Men can be modest and assume care-taking roles.
- Quality of life and a devotion to serving others are preferable to ambition and top performance.
- The group reacts permissively as long as a person's behavior is inconspicuous
- People sympathize with the weak.
- Average work performance is the norm.
- Failure when faced with high performance requirements is usually forgiven.
- Feelings of joy and sadness are expressed by both genders, i.e. men and women are both entitled pursue interpersonal relationships with sensitivity.
- Conflicts are settled through negotiation, **mediation** or compromise

In Western culture, a rather high **masculinity** index means that
- material success and progress are prevailing values
- money, objects, objective relationships and objective logic ("Aristotelian" thinking) play a predominant role

- men are often decisive, ambitious and tough
- women are generally sensitive and tend interpersonal relationships ("social networking")
- men cry less than women due to socialization and also, when attacked, fight back directly more often than women
- maximum work performance is the norm
- failure when faced with high performance requirements is often viewed as a catastrophe
- people sympathize with the strong
- people live to work
- superiors like to be decision-makers and make binding, clear decisions
- colleagues aspire to values such as performance, fairness and competitions among one another
- **disputes** are settled directly through confrontation

Now, we turn to the relatively weak **uncertainty avoidance** index in Southern Africa. It is much lower than that in Western countries such as Germany. Encounters with people from Southern Africa will likely involve the following factors:
- people are less likely to insist on their point of view, tolerance for ideas and opinions of others is important
- people are not looking for an absolute truth or a way to confront those with different religious views
- timeliness and precision are not particular expectations, they need to be learned
- aggressive behavior only occurs among peers, but not with superiors
- there is no great need for formal rules, neither at work nor in other areas of society
- people accept ambiguous situations with various risk levels
- stress symptoms are rather rare, leading to a frequent sense of subjective well-being

- it is undesirable to show aggression and certain emotions
- other people or outsiders are considered strange and are cause for astonishment
- time is merely a framework for orientation
- chatting, strolling about and nonchalance create a general sense of well-being
- differing opinions and ideas are tolerated
- motivation for work comes from the level of esteem and social requirements

People from Western cultures often find it important to avoid **uncertainty** in their life and work context if at all possible. This attitude means that the insecurity inherent in life and the incalculability of imponderables are viewed as a constant threat which must be fought or minimized through "insurance". This basic psychological state is expressed as follows:

- other people or outsiders are considered dangerous, yet sometimes as an adventure
- ambiguous situations and uncertain risks are avoided or "insured", while calculable risks are accepted
- differing ideas and behavior are usually considered exotic and often suppressed
- the motivation for work and other actions is promoted by the fulfillment of the security requirements
- timeliness, cleanliness and precision are crucial and generally accepted values
- there is a emotional need for activity and hard work
- there is a emotional need for rules, even if they do not work or are superfluous
- aggression and emotions can be shown in numerous situations and even during work

- individual and societal stress also creates a subjective sense of angst
- time is money

The overview provided here reveals latent tension and conflicts which can easily occur when people from Western cultures interact with people from Bantu-oriented cultures in Southern Africa. Focusing attention on culture-related dispute potential does not make the latent problem manifest. This qualitative leap depends on the critical mass of conflictive elements and the personal cultural expertise of the parties involved (see Chapter 6.1). Another factor also plays a role: intercultural conflicts decrease with more time spent in another cultural context and when the parties in conflict devote more effort to understanding the other cultural context. In general, experience has shown that low-conflict and, consequently, satisfactory cooperation can be achieved after six months of intercultural learning.

5.3 African conflict management in the context of Southern Africa

Since harmony and balance in interpersonal relationships are important and desirable values in traditional African cultures, it is foreseeable that the strongest option for action in conflict situations is **avoidance**. Intercultural disputes are ignored until the person involved poses an astonishing question about the object of conflict in the presence of the conflict parties or until complains to a trustworthy person. In rare cases, however, one of the conflict parties may address the problem directly, but this is considered impolite.

A special field which Westerners must deal with nearly every day is traditional African **conflict management.** While disputes in the West are usually dealt with personally and openly between the two parties, settled through extra-judicial means or through formal legal action, the traditional African calls for other basic forms of conflict management. For example, conflicts in the Swahili culture are frowned upon and considered a threat to group harmony. Utmost care is taken to avoid any conflicts at all between members of an *in-group*. If disputes do occur, however, they are usually settled indirectly through triangulation (see Chapter 4.1). If there is a conflict between management and employees, African workers usually take objective controversy personally. Therefore, an objective conflict generally means that the employee involved loses face. However, that is just the thing to be avoided according to traditional African thinking. Especially in Southern Africa, it is common in open and emotional conflict situations for other African colleagues to **tacitly** ally themselves (show "solidarity") with an employee in conflict with a Western manager. That may result in government or municipal authorities accusing the manager of being insensitive to the African citizens. As a consequence, the manager could even be expelled from the country as a *persona non grata* by the Immigration Office. This action by the authorities would resolve the conflict which had such a lasting effect on the orientation of the in-group.

Other traditional African means of dealing with conflict involve the **retreat** of people who, for example, feel they have been passed by or hurt. Sometimes, Africans act as if they are doing the opposite of what the instructions and rules dictate or disappear completely from any interaction. All these behavior options are respectable alternative from an emic point of view. Then, it is up to the mediators to deal with this very problematic situation.

The idea that overt conflicts must be **suppressed** is very widespread in Southern Africa, since overt conflict disturbs the harmony of relationships. As soon as a conflict is out in the open—this refers to the conflict style—some recognized people intervene who feel compelled to repress the conflict or at least put the conflict style into a more culturally compatible mode.

Another culture-spanning option in Southern Africa calls for **shifting** the conflict to other parties. This generally takes place through indirect or sometimes even direct blaming of other in-groups, ethnic groups and former colonizers in Southern Africa. In the latter version of conflict shifting, the injustices suffered during colonial times play a major role: Westerns, Brits and Boers are blamed for current conflict situations although there is very little or no connection to the current situation. That way, it is possible to stabilize and reconstruct relationships in an intercultural conflict situation dominated by traditional African ways of thinking.

Now, let's turn to the typical **conflict resolution styles** common throughout Southern Africa and, therefore, practical and advisable in intercultural conflicts. The first thing to note is that direct discussion between the people involved in the conflict only occurs in rare cases because direct forms of expression are usually considered strange and hurtful. That means that solutions are more readily developed through group consensus. As we saw above, the consensus method for resolving conflicts in Southern Africa is compatible with the prevailing cultural paradigm and is desirable. This consulting assembly is called the **Shauri** in Eastern Africa and the **Indaba** in Southern Africa. These assemblies of small groups develop solutions and present them to the conflict parties. The conflict parties give their approval since the collective has worked out the solutions. (Mayer 2003) An important point to note here is that this method does not involve any personal means of conflict resolution. In the business world, this style is of paramount importance because an intercultural conflict is sometimes attributed to a single person—at least on the surface. In general, there is a whole group of people behind one person. If one manages to bring the entire group to a consensus over the conflict, the solution will likely be more sustainable.

In the predominantly hierarchical cultures of Southern Africa where people blindly accept their place in the social web, there is another option for resolving conflicts: an authority intervenes, makes a decree and puts the conflict parties in their place.

The means of resolving conflict from the authoritative **power play** to mediating conflicts—in other words, the common forms of traditional African conflict resolution— are fluid. For people involved in resolving conflicts are usually representatives of religious, ethnic or clan-based groups. They are generally qualified and have enough life experience to successfully apply various conflict resolution styles in a culturally compatible manner.

5.4. Typical Conflict Situations between Westerners and Africans

Conflict situations between Westerners and Africans typically occur when the cultural worldview of the activity in the situation.
A look at the different orientations people have with regard to material property in everyday life reveals conduct which is obviously incompatible with corresponding attitudes among Westerners. A common problem is the natural tendency of most people in Southern Africa to borrow **possessions** or **property** belonging to public or private owners. Movable property in schools and businesses is especially targeted by this phenomenon. In many Southern African countries, it is apparently generally acceptable for employees to borrow tools, books and all sorts of other vital objects from schools and businesses and to use these object for their own purposes. If there are no clear rules set by the person in charge and the movable objects are not obviously locked up and kept under watch, people usually take that as a signal that material is "free" for anyone to use. The people's motive is not to steal when they handle property in this way —as Westerners often presume. Their motive is a temporary transfer of title on "call" for people who need to secure their survival.

By the same token, the term "corruption" must be viewed in this light. "Corruption" is traditionally unknown in Africa. There are just more or less broad rights of use which can be asserted depending on status and access options. However, if a clearly definable limit of culturally acceptable "use" of public property has been crossed, then that use turns into abuse which may be subject to corresponding punishment. In African church, municipal and ethnic communities, drawing the lines is often a source of major problems. Conflicts are likely to occur in situations where the completely different Western cultural definition of private and public "property", which always seems to be an expression of **power relationships**, clashes with the Southern African concept of treating property in areas of intercultural cooperation.

If the traditional African concept of use and usufruct is taken as a legitimization for a needy group to take possession of an object, there is an implicit factor for a certain cultural paradigm of **give and take**. Africans find it quite natural to give something from their surplus, to share what they have. It is hardly possible for Africans with high-paying jobs to avoid sharing their income with their extended family according to a clever system of distribution.

From a traditional African perspective, **sharing** is an obligation. The principle of "communal sharing" (Fiske according to Triandis 1994) is the term for this form of social behavior: "This kind of social behavior is valid in the families of many cultures. If the appropriate resources are available, people share according to their needs."

In contrast, from a Western perspective the owner solely and freely disposes of their own property.

As for the "motive" for **asking** for something, it is natural behavior in the culture of Southern Africa and also documented in several places in Holy Scripture. Asking and receiving, sharing possessions to satisfy basic needs is not only a reflection of the economic antagonism between wealth and poverty; it is also a basic religious tenet representing an ethical imperative for both Muslims and Christians. For example, in the Gospel according to Luke (11:9-10) reads: *"Ask, and it will be given you; search, and you will find; knock and the door will be opened for you. For everyone who asks receives, and everyone who searches finds, and for everyone who knocks, the door will be opened."*

This reference to a religious dimension possibly is likely an expression of African religiousness.

The act of asking in a traditional African cultural context is usually aimed at (symbolic) sharing and participation, and is not primarily a result of trade or borrowing. It is quite possible that—in cases where a Westerner would pay money in advance or borrow goods—an ownership claim or right of use is implied on the African side. Therefore, the borrowed objects are frequently used and/or consumed, rather than returned, since there is a need to be met.

Apparently, the cultural paradigms for **possessions and property** explained here are very much in effect even in low-key intercultural encounters and often lead to many conflicts. A relevant study on this topic (Boness 2002) shows that the success rate for intercultural mediation when dealing with divergent cultural paradigms on property issues is less than 50%. This relatively low rate is probably best explained by the fact that intercultural conflicts concerning possessions and property are quite often related to power relationships. Although the one-sidedness of the uneven power relationships between Westerners and Africans may have diminished in the recent past, the collective conscience of many Southern Africans is scarred by a feeling of inferiority in light of the superior behavior of Westerners experienced in cultural overlap situations.

Because **identity formation** in Southern Africa is collective rather than autonomous or individualistic, many Africans tend to have prejudices and stereotype the egocentric behavior of Westerners: Westerners are often seen as selfish and inconsiderate. From a Westerner's point of view, on the other hand, Africans seem incapable of forming an opinion of their own, making their own decisions and being independent.

This conflictive value constellation frequently gives rise to shifted conflicts because the conflict parties think ethnocentrically and judge everything according to their own perspective. Even though this may be the case, the conflict parties are usually completely oblivious to their own ethnocentric standpoint. Based on the assumption that projective perception of foreign cultures is a main characteristic of ethnocentrism, the following presents a few other important, yet hidden, cultural paradigms which affect the concrete conflicts at the tip of the iceberg.

The area of **status and ranking** which provide a party with their legitimization for acting and deciding is also subject to a broad range of cultural interpretations. From the African perspective, status and ranking are determined by birth, e.g. high status for someone with a chieftain's lineage or a shamanist clan. The cultural implication here is that African are mainly attributed their respectable social positions through higher birth or through relation to someone of high rank. From a Western perspective, Africans rely little on performance but use all kinds of nepotism to open doors. This often results in conflicts revolving around Westerners mainly focusing on effectiveness and productivity and only reluctantly agreeing to African recommendations to fill well-paid positions in a business with some people from a renowned, yet non-performance-oriented, extended family. These very contrary orientations often create conflicts which require mediation or consulting in order to continue satisfactory cooperation and interaction between Westerners and Africans.

More sporadic encounters between Westerners and Africans—short-term encounters, for example—the conflicts are usually in the area of Culture 1. Intercultural conflicts arise when Westerners

- do not wear the proper attire for the cultural context, wearing "comfortable" clothes instead
- dispense with greeting rituals and come right to the topic at hand
- do not bring along the anticipated guest gifts
- are poorly informed about the proper way of addressing their communication partners
- are ignorant of eating and drinking rituals and instead "dig right in"

- leave too little time to build personal relationships. Once an intercultural relationship is established, it often lasts for years.

From interviews, informal discussions and remarks on the side, it is clear that Africans and Westerners have a definite image of one another. These images and generalizations may contain a "kernel of truth", but are primarily misleading and can also fuel intercultural conflicts.

It should be noted that the following descriptions cannot to learned as recipes for the "right" way to behave in another cultural context. Rather, this background information serves as a means for Westerners to learn from the perceptions collected by other people who have been exposed to bicultural settings for an extended time. Behavior can only be sensitized, thereby reducing the risk of "reverting"to hetero- and auto-stereotypes and defusing intercultural conflicts, by becoming aware of one's own personal character traits and cultural attitudes in the context of mutual **stereotypes**. The provocative and conflict-inducing aspect of forming reciprocal stereotypes is that Westerners express precisely these stereotypes in interactions, in other words they use their stereotypes overtly and directly to explain events. However, Africans, who are just as zealous at maintaining their stereotypes, express themselves very rarely during interactions since they are acting in the interest of politeness, decency and verbal magic. In the context of action, though, they definitely express what they think of "Westerners".

Foreign stereotypes which are very hurtful to the African ear are the product of value judgments. Some of these stereotypes are part of the following **fictitious** mini-monologue which an ethnocentric Westerner might hold if asked what Africans are like.

"**Africans** are kind of dumb, they need to have everything explained to them three times. And they're much too polite, since it takes them forever to get to the point, while they talk about how their home is and how their relatives are. All the while, they seem pretty receptive, or even "passive", I would say. Africans only spring to action when there's something for free or if it's a matter of life and death. Other Westerners consider Africans idle and lazy, nothing gets going unless a white person is around and tells everyone what needs to be done. As soon as you turn your back, the Africans are right back to their old tricks. There are plenty of examples, just look at all the development projects which have been unsuccessful. And they are only concerned with one thing: money. They are always asking about money, and if they borrow some, they never give it back. They aren't trustworthy and can't manage their money very well. That's why they usually only enough money to get them through the day. They simply don't care about tomorrow. Yeah, they can throw a party. They know how to enjoy life better than we do in the West. But if someone is caught stealing, the party's over. Thieves are lucky to get away with their life. And how about those African women. They work practically morning, noon and night, raise the kids, work for a little bit of money and then even look after their men who usually sit around doing nothing. African women deserve much higher pay than they get."

Foreign stereotypes by Africans about Westerners can also be harmful to those from a Western cultural context. Here is a **fictitious** monolog from an African perspective.

"Why do Westerners have to follow their rules so closely and give such strict instructions when there are others ways to work? Westerners never seem to have any time, they can never wait and shove their way ahead instead of staying calm and letting things take their course. But work is one thing they can do. They work so hard, as if work could give their life a purpose. At least they're nice enough to share their know-how and information so we can learn a lot from them. One thing they don't have is trust in letting African run things. Instead, they stand around being critical and check up on everything and everyone. They are usually well prepared in projects and at seminars and very precise. It's surprising they can't keep their emotions under control, they scream, scold people, complain, accuse others of wrongdoing and are make to quick to pass judgment on things they don't even know about. All the while, they feel superior and treat you like an underling. Many

Westerners seem very unsure of themselves when they come to Africa. No wonder, since they don't learn from any of things they experience when they're here. They never go out of their way to get to know you and your family. They only see you as someone doing his job. They seem obsessed with making a good Westerner out of you. The more Westerners working on a project, the more problems there are in my experience."

This section concludes with further comment of the specific stereotypes which Westerners and Eastern Africans likely have of one another. These remarks are useful for refuting the above-mentioned projections and stereotypes in advance. According to our experience, however, hardly anyone could do without the relieving function of stereotypes when living and working in a foreign culture. Even so, Westerners would do well to come to terms with their own and foreign stereotypes in order to acquire a certain level of intercultural expertise (see Chapter 6.1) and facilitate mutually satisfactory cooperation with their African employees.

5.5 African Cultural Paradigms and their Effects on Western-African Mediation Processes

The relationship to **nature and the environment** for people with a traditional African orientation is primarily defined by the premise that God (in Swahili "*Mungu*") is the creator of all animate and inanimate things. Numerous myths about creation show that God is considered the former, creator and maintainer of nature.

This orientation to the environment can basically be seen in two different ways. Humans live in the environment and procure their subsistence from it, often from nature with much effort. Therefore, Africans experience their natural environment as a gift from God but also not always as a friendly counterpart. This basic attitude is common despite the sharp increase in urbanization tendencies in Southern Africa. Furthermore, this orientation seems to refer to both natural and social environments. The natural environment and the social environment are considered hierarchical systems of more or less animate things with respect to which humans must behave differently. In addition, based on this the assumption can be made that especially mid-range animate entities are not considered or defined as objects. They are seen as counterparts which God has provided as food to humans through providence. By the same token, some animals, especially doves, white chickens and white cows, are often considered and sent as carriers of spiritual forces and messages or used as sacrificial animals because they have a "spiritual overload". In a hierarchy of animate things, the collection of "vital forces", starting from the top down, is as follows:

God -> ancestors -> humankind -> animals -> plants -> matter

This system of various degrees of animation is based on a closed vision of the cosmos. If an element of the energized universe loses its vital forces, then another element gains the same amount of force (Teffo 1998). There is no distinction made between organic-animate and inorganic-inanimate elements in this concept of "vital forces".
In summary, it can be said that people with a traditional orientation have great respect for animated nature across all religious interpretations of nature and act according to the degree of animation with respect to the phenomena in their environment. However, that does not means that their actions are "environmental" or they have an "environmental conscience" is the Western sense. It is more probable that many Africans have no problem with their environmental actions and prefer to blame things like pollution on industrialized Western societies with their mass production and atomic reactors.

A common saying in Swahili culture goes: *"Maji yakija kwa nguvu yaache yapishe"* (i.e. "When waters comes with force, let it pass"). In other words, Africans are deeply aware of their dependency. Therefore, they try to deal with their environment as harmoniously as possible. This way of thinking about nature and the environment could be explained further with regard to cultural and social environments, but it should be noted that only in rare case do people have an attitude similar to the one in Western cultures which professes that humans should dominate, rule and/or exploit the environment for their own purposes.

This common Western attitude is foreign to most Africans for the simple reason that all human, cultural and social life, nature and the cosmos owe their existence to spiritual forces. Therefore, it should be assumed that Africans have grown up with a spiritual orientation which encompasses all things past and present.

Increasingly, people find themselves in intercultural situations where a lack of knowledge about **spiritual** perceptions of the world and the environment leads to tension and conflict between Westerners and Africans. Based on a few basic Swahili terms, we will now attempt to illuminate the thinking behind this phenomenon which is somewhat difficult for Westerners to comprehend. The collective experience of human dependencies in time and natural space leads to the concept of the **divine relationship**. Africans would have a hard time imagining not following the guidance provided by the knowledge of God's omnipresence. To date, there are practically no examples of "atheist" lifestyles disconnected from God. Indeed, there is no direct Swahili equivalent for the term "atheism". On the contrary, "Mungu" (i.e. "divine being") is the ontological origin and maintainer of the world. The majority of Africans do not really understand the grappling in major religions with the question of the true God and the true path to finding God. In a region with numerous indigenous religious forms where Christianity, Hinduism, Judaism and Islam have been culturally adapted, the embedment of being in the divine context is visible in everyday life. "Roho" (i.e. "the spirit") is also understood as a spiritual force which is the very thing that gives vital force to humans in the first place (Taasisi 1981). Africans do not see God as an anthropomorphic being. They see God as a "force" which functions dynamically in all things. There is very little graphic imagery of God, although God is worshipped for his role as a protector of family and ruler over the prosperity of human beings and animals. The common greeting or way of addressing a letter in Southern Africa is "Peace in the name of God", and people naturally bid farewell by saying

"God bless you". In other words, the beginning and the conclusion of events are placed in the hand of God. This invocation of God, in the sense of a divine force regardless of religious affiliations, expresses the wish that God might be present to accompany human beings in imponderable situations. Therefore, Westerners often find it disconcerting when the Southern Africans they are working with seem to place more trust in God than in the technical capabilities of experts or managers.

These cultural paradigms have a considerable effect on intercultural mediation. Mediation in African contexts often begins with a brief moment of silence, a prayer, singing or a creed. In general, the interveners or mediators ask for God's help before dealing with the matter at hand. Even so, these traditional African digressions or appeals to a higher power never smack of missionization for those present. Religion in Southern Africa is simply not a private matter for people have choose one belief or the other. The traditional African religious orientation is actually a basis for being and prayer is collective affirmation that those gathered are connecting to their mutual spiritual force.

People in sub-Saharan cultures also have a different **concept of time** than the Western-style concept of linear time. Traditional African cultures see people and/or groups as dependent variables of spatiotemporality living in deep dependency in a world of spiritual energies. Swahili culture, for example, offers a number of main concepts with regard to time and space which convey a sense of how most Africans view the world (Boness 2002).

The everyday terms most closely connected with spatiotemporality are "nafasi" and "kitambo" (i.e. "span of time" or "approximate distance") (Taasisi 1981). It is nearly impossible to explain all of the many context-related uses for "nafasi", but the term "nafasi" is used in communications variously as "opportunity", "place", "space", "frame", "capacity".

Westerners often find it difficult to understand the intentions of the speaker when there is time, for example, but *vice versa* no space. The use of "nafasi" is significant if it is used primarily to define a relationship. For instance, "Sina nafasi" (i.e. "I don't have any *nafasi.*") can mean that time and space are available, but the personal relationship between the people communicating with one another is not harmonious or not wanted. Westerners who try to translate the concept of on-time punctuality to Swahili are frustrated by the semantics: there is no translation for "**punctuality**". There is no equivalent term for this minor virtue in Swahili. One attempt at a translation for "punctuality" can be found in "kutochelewa" (i.e. "not delayed, not missing out"), which is a negative passive construction. Or English and Swahili are mixed, producing the sentence "hali (tabia) ya kuwa *punctual;* ya kufika wakati hasa upasao" (Johnson 1978). A literal translation of this is "the situation (the behavior), of being *"punctual"*—i.e. a translation which still does not yield a meaning for "punctuality" from a Swahili perspective, or "arrive at a time (see above) which is especially appropriate/fitting" — i.e. an adaptation which emphasizes the social contract aspect of "punctuality". With the penetration of Western time concepts in the areas of institutional cooperation or, to a limited degree, the modern transportation sector, people sometimes deal with two interpretations at once. It is a common for buses, taxis and other modes of public transportation to depart only when they are full, in other words much "too late" or even "too early", while others follow the timetable.

For mediation, this means that mediation sessions do not necessarily start on time, even if a place, date and time have been agreed. The "fitting" appearance of African conflict parties goes according to how important the mediation is for those involved, as well as according to the social ranking of the particular conflict party. The higher someone is in the social, economic, religious or seniority hierarchy, the more "time" they can take to show up. Therefore, difficulties arise when Western oriented mediators plan too little time for intercultural mediation since time is more fluid for Africans.

A number of African cultures lack an appropriate word for "future" altogether. Instead, the present time (in Swahili "*Sasa*") and the past (in Swahili "*Zamani*") are successive, retrospective areas which signify the course of life for Africans. The present time includes all significant events in life which are currently occurring, have recently occurred or are about to occur. There is no appropriate time dimension called the "future" since events in the future have not yet occurred. One exception to this are predetermined events reflecting the cycles of nature such as rainy season, birth and death. People from a traditional African cultural context deal with events that are occurring now or which have occurred in the past and effect present action. They "...are only mildly or not at all interested in events which lie more than two years in the future..." (Mbiti 1974:23). In fact, when Africans talk about something like "eternity", they use the expression "in the past and in the ancient past ". That means extending a hardly remembered past even further "back".

While Westerners tend to have a rather **one-dimensional** (monochromic) understanding of time, thereby concentrating on one task at a certain time with a predefined time frame, Africans usually see time in **multiple dimensions** (polychromic). They handle several tasks at once, focusing more on the maintenance and formation of social relationships than on dates and deadlines. Africans are more amenable to revising plans and taking specifications "lightly". This also relates to another conflict in attitudes since Westerners tend to see time in set linear terms. The implication of this Western attitude can be seen in starting meetings on time, taking deadlines seriously and the ability to complete tasks on short notice. Much to the contrary, most Africans perceive time as a multiple fluid continuums, crisscrossing one another and then separating again. The departure of a bus or the start of work at the office depends on whether the people are ready. People prefer to complete tasks without a set schedule and delays are considered a normal part of life.

In the context of conflict management in the mediation process, these traditional African cultural paradigms mean that the conflict parties prefer to discuss and work on several conflict points at once. They have no problem with "saving" a conflict point, which might be quickly settled in Western oriented mediation, for the next session or the session after next. Conflict points are approached in the present and in correlation with the requirements of the past. Events and plans are subject to a compatibility test to determine the degree to which they violate tradition, customs and traditional African values. These world views clearly show the problems and conflicts that can occur when Westerners interact on the basis of future-oriented action. Most people with a Western world view find it important to determine the future use of a plan where long-term consequences and success play a role. The traditional African concepts of time have a much different effect on mediation. Life oriented to the present and past means that Southern Africans judge events and plans and the changing thereof mainly according to the short-term benefits or the short-term success. However, it should be noted that up-and-coming generations in Southern Africa are thinking more of the long-term effects of their present actions for their current activity.

Keeping before our eyes the survey just presented on the application and perception of time dimensions, we readily understand that, especially in situations of interaction between Westerns and Africans, the semantic and practical divergences of concepts of time can lead to numerous conflicts, misunderstandings, and false interpretations.

When Europeans wend their ways to Africa, they come from a cultural context that is actively behavior-oriented. The predominant cultural orientation to "action" stresses accomplishment, attainment of one's goals, and improvement of one's own living standard. Even one's leisure time is thoroughly "animated," vacation activities" are announced, one keeps moving. Africans often see Europeans as "hard-working people," then, who simply never find any leisure for repose, reflection, and meditation. This stereotype is stubborn as a mule. Southern Africa's own perception of activity lies in emphasis on the instant, which ought to be as pleasant as possible, and convey the feeling of well-being. Africans approach actions and behavior with an attitude

Europeans regard as "passive." But this kind of orientation to behavior occasions contentment and relaxation, in work and personal life alike. Even when guests from Europe pay a visit, the African hosts are concerned to focus their activities, so that guests may enjoy as contented an atmosphere as possible, at social encounters, at work, at meals, and at festivals. Africans are very conscious of the fact that this kind of satisfaction and quality of life are strongly motivating for current projects, and a consensual creation of decision. Atmosphere is an essential component--so to speak, an existential quality--of Southern Africa. In situations of mediation, it can become quite difficult if Europeans stress their own model, that of achievement, and active management of conflict solutions or agreements. Most Africans are "partial to" a good atmosphere. In intercultural mediation, "feeling comfortable" is not only a prerequisite for "getting active", it is also the goal to be reached at the end of the mediation.

From the African perspective, the particularities of communicative action, and the underlying structure of communication, play a salient role in mediation. In the literature, it is designated as "high context" communication. Most Africans have need of a high measure of contextual information about their partners, before either any business, or "thing-oriented" association, can be begun at all. In other words, interpersonal episodes are erected and developed upon personal relationships. This circumstance frequently leads to considerable irritation in Westerns, who shape, for example, their business relationships, impersonally instead. There is simply no necessity of being up to date regarding the family, or personal circumstances, of business associates. Information of material interest is explicitly exchanged, verbally and in writing. How differently flows the communication of African business partners! They apply very strongly nonverbal signals, expressed in tone of voice, body language, facial expression, eye contact, and the intentional application of pauses in speech. Africans prefer to communicate indirectly. Verbal communication typically flows by way of proverbs, sayings, and Old African idioms.

The necessary material information is drawn from the social network, which is difficult for Europeans to penetrate. Possible effects on the situation of mediation lie ready to hand: Conflicting African parties will tend to carry on a lively conversation enriched with personal questions and family stories. One is inclined to seek a better personal acquaintance, before entering the series of problems. The social context is, as it were, the foundation on which rests the house of conflict-management in common. The more stable the foundation, the more probable are durable outcomes and agreements in the mediation. It is for these essential variants of culturally specific orientation to communication that intercultural mediators must be ready and prepared, especially when a Western-oriented party would like to "come right to the point," and prefer to omit family stories and histories as "private matters."

Further forms of communication among Africans consist in the indirect communication of conflicts, mostly dealt with through "go-betweens." No need exists to extend conflicts with open confrontation, since one side could then lose face. Europeans are often "tricked" by a feeling that African conversation partners are too cowardly to settle the conflict, or even that they are "wrong," if they invoke third parties for intervention. But it is precisely this African "triangulation" of a conflict that often contributes so powerfully to a pleasant atmosphere--because of a third party "helping out."

Communication in Southern Africa—and this phenomenon is very puzzling at first glance—often proceeds emotionally, and allows for the recognition of feelings. Body language is clear, although only practiced among partners of the same sex. The African side quickly takes its distance from a participant who conveys expressions of tenderness toward someone of the other sex, or even presumes merely to offer a friendly embrace. Corporal communication of this sort belongs to the area of the most intimate family relationship: that of spouses, and even then it is not practiced publicly in an intercultural situations. In the emotional atmosphere specific to the culture of Southern Africa, only certain feelings are considered appropriate in public communication. Joy and enthusiasm may be expressed by laughing, or by culturally specific forms. For example, in East Africa women express their enthusiasm or agreement with a high-pitched tremolo of the tongue, onomatopoeically called vigelegele. In certain situations, it is permitted to express grief loudly and openly. The expression of astonishment usually indicates a perception of strange behavior, one that fails to correspond with one's own orientations. In Southern Africa, it is regarded as most impolite to express annoyance, chagrin, anxiety, stress, tension. This makes it understandable that certain conflicts between Europeans and Africans are expressed emotionally. No European may allow him/herself to express irritation, or to upbraid, when something "is not going as it ought." Such an emotional form of expression would occasion the unhesitating perception among Africans that the European involved lacks all respect for Africans, and wantonly offends the honor of the family, the village, or even the whole culture. The restoration of intercultural relations that have thus eroded is a long process. Probably such restoration will be achieved only through a form of intercultural mediation that reacts most sensitively to taboos, and to adjustments of emotional expressions, and that involves "excuse" and "forgiveness" in its meaning for the African-oriented party to the conflict.

Finally, it will be in order to indicate a form of communication, specific to Africa, that, especially for us Westerns, is not readily perceptible. Which path of communication, the more formal, or the more informal, is to be chosen, when one wishes to set up and maintain a good relationship?

When we consider the culturally differentiated styles of negotiation between us, it becomes strikingly clear how strange an effect it must have on Europeans when the African side prefers to avail itself of informal relations, in order to gather a sense of what the negotiations will be about. Negotiations frequently collapse when it is not the recognition and analysis of data and facts that is at issue, not a rationally intelligible, structured process that is aimed at. What Africans prefer is that there be good relations, and that any negotiation proceed on this basis. This costs time, particularly when it is clear to all concerned that the connection of numbers and data, of profit expectations and coefficients of productivity, proceeds more rapidly and more easily than the connection of people who intend to cooperate with one another.

What is normative for the informal path of communication is the degree of openness of a situation, and the equal "rank" of those in communication. Contemporary children, youth, and young adults, respectively, can communicate with the fewest complications. As soon as someone else enters the field of communication--someone who stands higher in the social hierarchy, has more power, plays a special role, or simply is older--the path of communication swerves. Now formal speech is used, and etiquette and manner of address is explicitly preserved. The majority of persons in the South of Africa tend to emphasize their own history, traditions, and cultural particularities. They are class and hierarchy conscious, and have a sense of a person's social position. This results in their stricter demand that "the protocol prescriptions "be observed with regard to social rank. For example, special rules hold for communication with clergy, officials, teachers, and employers. When the conflicting parties negotiate in the setting of an intercultural mediation, they will be well advised to ascertain usages and rites before they enter the situation of communication. In this manner, trust and sincerity will be generated on the African side because respectful conduct is positively observed.

As already mentioned, the question of relations with, and attitudes toward, authority among the cultures, is of central importance for intercultural conflicts. In Germany, authority is acquired, with political, economic, or other means, and attained through ability and self-responsibility, if not indeed by money, election, or party membership. For Africans, it looks as if authority were not gained, so much as ascribed. In this area, then, conflicts may arise, if, e.g., Europeans are struck by how incapable and corrupt many African authorities appear to them, be it in state offices, be it in the church, or in industry. Tribal politics plays an important background role, in numerous countries of Southern Africa, when it comes to the assignment of positions of authority, with the accompanying access to important resources. This role will frequently remain unidentified, and invisible, in conflictive situations of pressing importance. Instead, it is a role that must be brought to light, in processes of intervention, or in the mediation process. In intercultural situations, conflicts of authority play an extremely important role. On the African side, the conceptualization frequently resonates that Europeans have secured powerful authority over Africans, and that now they must return, so to speak, or share, their power in compensation. It is precisely this culturally specific, and widespread, opinion prevailing among Africans that Europeans all too often either ignore, or completely underestimate. On the surface, this intercultural paradigmatic constellation shows itself straightforwardly in property crimes, assaults, threats, and extortion. This sort of superficial conflict is only to be illuminated, of course, when it is recognized that an explosive mix of divergent orientations prevails with regard to authority, status, and rank, as well as social role. This mixture must be "factually fathomed," anew, in any situation of conflict.

By way of example, social roles in Southern Africa are defined and ascribed according to family membership, clan, or tribal membership. The basic requirement, in the upper reaches of social recognition, is that, according to the respective matrilinear or patrilinear structuring of each population group, there be persons who are experienced, and mature or elderly. Still today, a store of wisdom gathered over decades of life becomes the basis of high esteem. It is regarded as "capital," to be handed down to coming generations, and it plays a decisive role even in industrial and economic connections. Experience in living means power, and decision-making authority. Accordingly, Africans are astonished when they remark that a young Western, with very good special formation, receives a position that involves a great amount of personal decision-making. Here is a Western scarcely forty-years-old deciding over so many resources, and in charge of so many persons, when he does not have the necessary experience in life, in fact, often does not even have a family and children! Latent conflict and competition situations often arise on this point. This intercultural conflict of value constellations shows itself in hesitation in the mediation process, or even out-and-out non-cooperation.

African orientations to possession and property are closely bound up with the question of authority, and today come into ever sharper opposition to European conceptualizations. It is terrible to have to follow, in the media, the practical dispossession, expulsion, imprisoning, and even killing of so many white settlers and farmers who have tilled the soil for generations in Zimbabwe. This appears to Europeans as a great violation of rights. The British Zimbabwians have not only taken the land, but have acquired legal and valid property titles over it. The African families who work the farms stand, as a rule, in ongoing work relationships, and are now uprooted. In other South African countries, such power politics of dispossession have, in part, been criticized—not, however, in their goal: Europeans are welcome as guests, but not as possessors of land, or of mineral wealth. There are efforts in the international community, as well as projects of Western agencies of developmental cooperation, to soften this highly explosive potential for conflict, through the construction of civil structures, and the preparation of instruments of conflict settlement. The basis of these property conflicts is that, in the Southern African view, there is no such thing as concrete property. Thus, most Bantu languages make no distinction between possession and concrete property. For another thing, private property is intrinsically foreign to the African notion of possession. Only a group, family, or ethnic unit may use land, and not an individual. This revitalization of the Old African collective claim to a "right" increasingly marks public confrontation in Southern Africa. At the moment, it cannot be predicted which areas of economy and politics it will include, and there open new settings for cultural conflict.

As presented above, most population groups in Southern Africa are oriented collectivistically. They are typified by the subordination of individual interests to the interests of a community. A close group-connection protects the members, and demands loyalty and obedience in return. Social control is grounded on fear and sanctions, loss of face and shame. These characteristics, and more besides, relate to the basic unity of social forms, the family.

Almost all Africans feel obligated to their extraction, their forebears, their family. Here they are rooted, from here they come, from them they live, from them they relate to their cultural and personal support. If we investigate the relationship of individual persons in their community, it is obligatory to begin with the family, and not with the individual person. In numerous countries of Southern Africa, in applying for a visa, one's family name is, as it were, investigated. The examiner is told one's social and personal place, which follows one's line, into the past. Most often, in African daily life, we meet the extended family. An official government lexicon, for example, gives the information that the family (Swahili, jamaa) carries the primary meaning of "watu wa ukoo mmoja, ndugu", "person of a descendancy, a siblingship," (Taasisi, 1981). In a second meaning, jamaa includes persons of a common system of reference—persons, therefore, who belong to a social group or community having certain characteristics. In the concept of the state—and this is a third variant—the special concept of family echoes in a form broadened to include nation. For most Africans, this goes without saying, but we ought to emphasize it here, owing to the proprietary concentricity of the concept of family. In the large independent states, their "Founding Fathers" are essentially better known than the current rulers. It was the old, wise Fathers who have founded a national family and led it to independence. To name only a few: Kauna for Zambia, Nujoma for Namibia, Mandela for the Republic of South Africa, Mugabe for Zimbabwe, Nyerere for Tanzania, and Kenyatta for Kenya.

For Europeans, the fundamental applicability and effect of the concept of family in partial areas of societies is surprising. Numerous industries are built on the concept of family, its structure, hierarchy, and the decision-making process. Religious and confessional societal forms are often perceived and accepted as family, communications in addresses are likened to family addresses, inner order resembles the Old African family order. Nor is it astonishing, then, that, in Africans' understanding, family includes the souls of the dead, and the unborn, as an rigidly concentric circle. Thus, the present focus of the family is immediately connected with the no-longer and the not-yet within the "now" of the family. As a rule, contacts and communication with the "living dead" run connected with the patrilocal or matrilocal household. Around the circle of family households lies the circle of the neighborhood, which, it is true, affords a less obligating systems of contacts, but does contribute a community of the common life and mutual assistance.

Now, given that the Old African family today still presents its real and symbolical effectiveness as the basic unity of a collectivistic orientation, the question arises of what place the individual occupies in this cultural system of relations.

African researcher and philosopher Kwame Gyekye confronts the person and the concept of personality. He has presented his notion of each, in the framework of the Council for Research in Values and Philosophy (Coetzee 1998), before UNESCO. For him, against a background of political theory, it is predominantly society that determines the "'becoming-ness' of persons." Gyekye broadens the play of the concept of person by including the "nature-given attributes." For him, the person is defined through the "rights of the individual", through "duties towards others", and through the "appreciation of common life or collective good" (Gyekye 1992). He speaks of the "communitarian self", in which it is not through reason, will, or memory that the person is defined, but through community. According to Gyeke, this "communitarian concept of person" is composed in the following way. Human beings do not choose their society. They suddenly become the "cultural being" that cannot exist in isolation from other human beings. Instead, the person is oriented to others naturally. Social relationships, according to Gyeke, are necessary for the constitution of the person.

Person-becomingness must be learned, and can be failed, missed. A person's value system and aim in life, Gyeke says, are not unconditionally identical with those of the socio-cultural structure of the community. Rather, personal values condition the function of the structure, and influence it (Gyeke 1992). If the human being is affected by negative values, as by being "wicked," "bad," „ungenerous," "cruel." Or "selfish," then that human being is not a person, nor is there any possibility that s/he become a person. Among positive values, on the other hand, according to Gyeke, the Akan cite "generosity,""kindness,""compassion,""benevolence,""respect,""concern for others", "peacefulness", "humility", and "promotion of the welfare of others", with the last named representing the highest value. If a human being is designated as a person, this means, simultaneously, that s/he has a good character. "Personhood" can be measured only in moral categories, i.e., in moral qualities and capacities, and is thereby dependent on a moral judgment to be rendered by others. So the community places its centers of gravity on obligations rather than on rights, without suggesting any equivalency between them. Gyekye emphasizes a person's dual responsibility, which unites, he says, individual and collective rights. In this way, individual rights, e.g., equal treatment, property, freedom of speech and assembly, are recognized, provided the community can survive. If community goods are at stake, however, individual rights can be restricted or opposed by the community. Thus, the determination of rights, when all is said and done, remains in the hands of the community (Gyeke 1992).

For intercultural mediation procedures, the above-presented cultural orientations to individualism and collectivism, to person and community, are especially incisive. We may presuppose that not only a person, but the entire relational group of an African type conflictive party, feels injured and assaulted, as soon as one of the above-cited conflict-constellations enters between Western and African orientations. For the mediators, this circumstance means that, in a word, one person from Southern Africa does not form a conflicting party. That takes this person's whole relational group. Furthermore, a culturally specific concrete situation such as this can spark the entire relational group: now they may signal an interest in a mediation, in order to be there as a "rear guard", or to form a common field of force. If the relational group fails to appear, probably the mediation process will be considerably diminished in content, and delayed in time, since the relational group's authorities must first confront the particular position in which the conflict management is found. Here is the place to re-emphasize the "I"-form of address. The "I"-address, in intercultural mediation represents a disguised "we"-address. The collective responds through the individual person. As we have seen, the person, in an Old African perspective, is attributed some important positive values for the process of mediation. These introduce the needed relaxation, in order to conduct an intercultural conflict without "explosions" of wounded feelings.

Closely tied to orientation to activity is orientation to "contest." "Competition enlivens business, "we may say, to capsulize in a nutshell a widespread Western notion in social and economic contexts. An orientation to contest is signaled by an emphasis on achievement, self-assurance, and competition. The aim is the acquisition of material goods, money, or property. A positive estimation is made where ambition, achievement, decisiveness, speed, and quantity are in evidence.

What a contrast with Old African values of harmony and community thinking, solidarity and reciprocity! The Old African orientation is to cooperation, especially in the economic area, but also in the other social areas. As already mentioned above, in our elucidation of the cultural dimension of the "femininity" of Sub-Saharan cultures, empathy and cooperation with weaker co-workers mark the atmosphere. Harmonious relationships always have precedence over labor. Comparisons of individual accomplishment are very rare. They would "de-motivate," since individual persons would have the feeling of being "divided out" from the rest. Material encitements, then, succeed only on condition that they are placed not before the individual, but before the entire group. The capitalist system, with its imperatives of accomplishment and work, will probably be rather rarely accepted, nor even internalized, in Southern Africa. Conflicts arising from this often observed fact, then, have at most something to do with the divergent cultural orientations to contest and competition. Especially, the history of Southern Africa recounts numerous tragedies in labor conflicts played out between members of British populations and those of British extraction on the one hand, and the black population on the other. It is not least of all from these deep-lying experiences that any mediation centers have formed in the Republic of South Africa to this day, that take up and successfully manage labor conflicts.

African cultural orientations regarding order and structure involve arrangement, which is slow to be completed. If an order is to be erected, needs must first emerge. For example, complicated arrangements are set up in visits of an official kind, and a catalogue of points is drawn up, all of which lend the events an importance of their own kind. From time to time, rites and festivals are highly structured, and national and ethnic celebrations are conducted in strict forms, which frequently evokes the impression with Westerns that these festive occasions are truly very "stiff." Practically no space is left for structured communication, and the everyday returns to be dealt with. Thus, one meets very flexible orientations with respect to order and structure. Whether there are rules or not, it is possible to live without them, after all. A need for order in all areas of life is very little emphasized. As we have already worked out in our disquisition on the cultural dimension of "avoidance of the unsure," Africans behave essentially more tolerantly in unsurveyable situations, vis-à-vis unknown persons and ideas. On practical grounds, one takes care to achieve one's goal in, so to speak, in a "roundabout fashion," that is, through informal communication structures. For the mediation process, this flexible use of order and regular structures has the effect that, very probably, the classic Western model of phases is not very appropriate, since the phases, like the rules of speech, fail to meet the necessities of persons of an Old African orientation.

To describe special African orientations to styles of thought, which would be distinguished as somewhere between deductive and inductive, would really be very difficult. On the one hand, Africans reason inductively from the concrete. Then too, their observations and experiences flow into grand theories of the everyday, the world, and the divine. With most Africans, however, an interest in the value of enumeration and statistics for control of everyday life is not very marked. Instead, we shall probably meet with an orientation in thinking that can be grasped holistically. Working and thinking are not divided, but integrally related. Family and environment are not divided in cognition: they live together there in a reciprocal dependency. Even spiritual energy—as we have presented it above--is conceived and felt as a power that binds all being together, from "lifeless matter" to the "most alive" and vibrant divine Being. The purpose of being, and of human existence, the quest for truth and the meaning of life—all of these orientations, philosophically and theologically important for us, have far less meaning for Africans. Just as little has "Aristotelian logic" any connection with Old African styles of thinking. Thought runs not according to the rules of Western logic, but according to insight, and experience of insight, it runs into connections. From of old, the latter have been filled with meaning and handed on in images, histories, analogies, metaphors and idioms,

For intercultural mediation, African styles of thought "work," we might say, as follows. Events and occurrences that have been experienced conflictively, tend to be transmitted by the African conflicting party laden with images, and enriched with metaphors. It is important, then, on the part of the mediator, that s/he glance into the thought world of metaphors and idioms, in order to understand the underlying messages in a way that takes the culture into consideration, and to weave them into the conflict management.

In conclusion, we come to the cultural paradigm with respect to Old African causal attribution. We mean the kind and manner in which Africans indicate causes, bases, and consequences of certain events. One's own achievement or deed as cause or basis of good or bad results is less to be seen, than the Predetermined - many call it fate - that one so "capably performs." Obviously there are powers that more or less "collect" in a person, and render that person capable of something special--be it rain-making, healing, spell-casting--thus many Africans conceptualize it. When one achieves, one does not "pat oneself on the back", but rather, thanks those that have enabled one to perform accomplishments.

An example from everyday life shows beautifully how the Old African paradigm affects causal attribution. In the great rain season, the drainage system of a West African state no longer functions. The pipes are rusted away, stopped up, and overcome by the amount of rain. At first no one reacts (cf. Chap. 4.7). Instead, after a certain time, African experts in water magic, and elders with experience of the rainy season, are assembled. Together, these persons form a strong collectivity, that is then in a position - perhaps with the help of technicians - to influence the water system so that the bad energies that have led to the blockage are successfully expelled. The problem is solved not on the basis of the technological intervention—rather, the technical intervention can be successful only if the energies so flow that the supplementary technology will be able to fulfil its purpose.

For situations of mediation, these causal attributions, in the Old African conception, are effective in that it is not owing to the mediator, as a qualified go-between, that the intervention has succeeded, success nor even to the capable and cooperative conflicting partes, but to the energies summoned, in whose service the mediators and conflicting parties are placed. Thus, mediation sessions frequently begin with a prayer and brief silence, that the Spirit may favorably charge the space in and between the participants for the management of the matter at hand.

5.6 Possibilities for Mediation in Western-African Situations of Conflict

5.6.1 Examples of African Mediation in Intercultural Contexts

First let us consider possibilities of mediation as they are conducted in Western-African conflict situations by Old African personalities, that is, by persons who have undergone no Western formation in mediation. The following brief presentation also gives an impression of the status, age, social prestige, occupation, and gender of the African mediators.

During field research of several years in Tanzania, 408 intercultural interactions between Europeans and Africans (Boness 2002) were investigated. Among these cases, recalled and recounted by African authors alone, 87 explicitly describe intervention by mediators. Considering the success or failure of the intervention of mediators in encounters characterized by conflict, one can establish that, of the 87 interventions by cultural mediation, 77 led to positive outcomes, while 10 emerged in the negative.

Conflicts involving subsequent intercultural mediation principally involve divergent cultural orientation to "possession and property"(20 cases, of which 7 were unsuccessful), "outward appearance" of the person **(14 cases, of which 1** unsuccessful), foreign culture 1 (11 cases, all successfully mediated), "language"(9 cases, all successfully mediated), "education (8 cases, 1 unsuccessful). A more precise overview shows:

African Intercultural Mediation

Cultural Orientation to:	Number of cases of mediation with a positive outcome	Number of cases with a negative outcome
Labor and cooperation	1	
Possession and property	13	7
Education and learning	7	1
Sexuality	5	1
Alienation	11	
Health and illness	2	
Trade	3	
Consumption	2	
Authority (power) and conflict	4	
Person, outer appearance	13	1
Religion	1	
Speech and communication	9	
Environment	1	
Time and space	5	

Graph: Cultural Orientations

Negative outcomes despite African mediation are observed especially in the cultural category of possession and property: 7 out of 20. Interesting, in this connection, is who it is that volunteers for the task of mediator, and under what circumstances the mediation miscarries. Selected cases present the process:

One reporter depicts a situation in which his friend takes photographs of persons without being invited, and is designated a "thief." Despite intervention on the part of the African writer of the report, who acts as mediator in the case, the photographer is insulted by Tanzanian citizens. The attempt at mediation comes too late.

Another occurrence revolves, at bottom, around a division of meat. A European, passing a church with his hunting kill, is asked to give some meat to church members. He hesitates, even though the community leader explains to him why these requests are made. The Tanzanian mediator (the community leader) is rejected by the European hunter.

The distribution of clothing from a container of contributions is the subject of a mediation that comes to no result. The distributor, a European, proceeds strictly according to his criteria of distribution of contributions, and cannot accept it that there be other distribution needs, as are presented from the African side. The mediation of an older Tanzanian go-between, who throws further light on the petitioner's need, is basically unsuccessful.

In another case, a schoolteacher attempts to mediate a property crime, but does not succeed.

The violent encounter between a Western cashew-farmer and some thieves brings so much unrest into the village that the state intervenes, and expels the Western from the country. True, it was not a mater of a mediation in the strict sense, but rather of the state restoring social peace in the region, acting as an intervening third party—at the expense of the Western, however, who was in the right, according to the view of the African author.

With regard to the cultural paradigm of "a person's outward appearance", the case of a deficient mediation of teachers is reported, who, after lengthy discussions, could not put down pupils' "bad behavior".

Intercultural mediation indicates high success quotients in all areas listed except "possession and property". In the category, "labor and cooperation", a successful mediation is conducted by a leader of the Tanzanians, who encourages his reluctant compatriots to cooperate in the restoration of the water supply.

In the case of a theft, Tanzanian teachers succeed in their mediation, feeling responsible for their Western colleagues, and assuring the return of the stolen goods.

A "case of corruption" in a technological-formation establishment enables the author's friend to mediate with success, and restore willingness for mutual cooperation. A similarly structured case is successfully mediated by the involved party himself, by seeing to it that urgent medical care can be maintained, although essential instruments are "lacking." Especially successful is the intervention of Tanzanian friends of the Europeans who take photos without asking permission.

Even the police come into the situation, when there is question of a property crime, or of letting Europeans know that it is well to avoid taking pictures without the approval of both sides.

In the area of the cultural paradigm, "education": official representatives, or even "pupils," "Tanzanian hosts," or "teachers" - in particular cases even the accompanying teachers in a "school exchange" - contribute to the clarification of irritating encounters.

The very distant cultural paradigm in the area of "gender" contains cases like the one in which a "Coordinator for International Student Exchange" functions more as a counselor than as a mediator, taking protective measures against sexist machinations by Europeans.

A like protective function is perceived by a host, when s/he explains to his/her European guests that kissing in public does not fit in with African culture. Cultural conflicts in behavior are mediated in the area of "foreignness and contact" by, for example, the "person in charge" of a restaurant, who counters a discriminating rejection of a Tanzanian by a waiter. The in-between role of a teacher is on the same level, when he moves villagers to take a distance from the notion that Europeans are "bloodsuckers" or parasites. Fear of "black skin" is quieted with a mediator's reference to the completely normal differences in the "way people look". A bilingual person mediates the conflict between a Tanzanian taken into custody and the immigration police in an airport in Paris. Fellow students mediate between beggars and the European tourists. In another case, "loyal passengers" step in for a fair price for bus tickets, which Europeans and Africans alike are to pay.

A political chief of administration of a locale (in Swahili, mwenyekiti wa kijiji) successfully mediates a case ordered to the paradigm of criticism "power and struggle", a violent confrontation between a Western and the Tanzanian author, so that it comes down to the notion of the problematic behavior of the white party. Likewise, the director of a college succeeds in settling the quarrel between Tanzanian exchange students and French cleanup workers by paying the Tanzanians the respect due them.

The conflictive area of divergent cultural orientations to "speech and communication" is overwhelmingly characterized by the mediation being successfully managed by clarification at the hands of the "headmaster," or by the authors participating in the conflict. In the area of cultural displacements vis-à-vis "environment and nature", a bishop acts as mediator, who successfully influences the contra-productive activities of the Africans in the framework of a seminar for environmental protection.

A bicultural member of the Black African culture functions as mediator for the successful control of a conflict whose subject is "bodily proximity", which is variously interpreted in the different cultures, by elucidating for an irritated Tanzanian, who is abroad, the semantic particularities of bodily distance and proximity in Europe. Thereby he brings to resolution the conflict that has arisen. "Closeness to the teachers", practiced by the pupils in an English exchange delegation during its visit to Tanzania, is critically mediated by the Tanzanian hosts during a school exchange.

A conflict over the "punctuality" of Tanzanian public transportation is successfully resolved through the mediation of the "railroad station manager." The principal of a secondary school in Moshi successfully mediates the temporarily unsuccessful goodbye party, from which a European teacher has distance himself because of the schedule set up by the African friends, but not observed.

To sum up: we can conclude that, in the first instance, leading, elder personalities, as well as friends granted participation in the cultural intersecting situations, and "passers-by", cooperate in a successful or unsuccessful mediation. The high proportion of successful mediations indicates the importance of mediative cooperation in settings of intercultural conflict. At the same time, the high cultural acceptance and solidity of Old African mediation, for the purpose of the restoration of social harmony, is underscored. This is not always recognized by members of Western culture. Many Europeans, as we have seen above, reject a mediation session. Report indicating a culturally specific management of "possession and property" lie well forward in the frequency of unsuccessful mediations. One-third of attempted mediations in this area are unsuccessful. It may be supposed that no simple regulations of conflict can be found situatively. According to the reports of the African writers, culturally strongly deviating sensitivities and conceptualizations are appeased.

5.6.2 Foundations of Western-African Mediation Settings

Persons introduced as mediators in situations of European-African conflict are subject to elevated requirements. Mediation plays out not only in conflicts in one's own cultural frame of relationships, but holds a special depth structure: the mental structure of a foreign, distant culture. It is especially worth re-emphasizing the latent empowerment imbalances prevailing in various areas, which must be sensitively grasped and leveled out. When an intercultural mediation is requested, then, or is evinced as necessary, it is worth verifying what presuppositions must be developed individually, in order to create the conditions for the possibility of a successful Western-African mediation.

First, the question must be asked, what place is favorable for a mediation: it is a matter of the atmosphere at the beginning of the procedure. From the African viewpoint, it can very well be the place in which the conflictive event occurs or has occurred. That is uncomplicated, and especially precedes the restoral of relations before other activities. Accordingly, a neutral place is not the necessary prerequisite for conducting a Western-African mediation. But it is also altogether possible to seek out the place in which the mediating personality dwells. Everything that we know about African cultural orientations to locations, is the fact that spaces designated as private by us Western-oriented persons are regarded by Africans as semi-public. Consequently, a correspondingly formal situation of communication prevails there that is highly prized on the African side. Official formality strengthens the African parties to the conflict in the security of their roles. This includes the talks - in the case of youth, with given names and position in formation, with adults their function and institutional connections - and their location in the family structure. Interaction becomes possible, exchange of information concerning children, parents, relatives, common acquaintances--in a word, a "high context" communication is striven for, at least in the approach, in order to promote the comfort of the conflicting parties.

Then the "dynamic neutrality" of the mediator must be determined. This is the key to trust. For Africans, primarily mediators or arbitrators are acceptable, who are significantly older. In the Old African semantics, this means that, where at all possible, making persons available who bring along a corresponding competency in experience of real life, adjustment, and wisdom, which constitute a cultural precondition for a /winning course of mediation. It turns out to be an effective and respectful measure when the, e.g., Western mediator sits alongside a counterpart from the African culture. The counterpart helps mot only to strengthen the African side, but also to transmit the very diverse cultural semantics by way of her/his own cultural competency.

Regarding the role of mediator, the following difference obtains vis-à-vis mediation in the Western context. Here, the mediators are regarded as protectors and guardians of the proceeding, and the conflicting parties solve the dispute themselves in such a safeguarded framework. In the Western-African situation, matters have another cast. Since mediators tend to be persons of a relatively high age/status, it is correspondingly expected, of their mature wisdom, that they enter the process lending moderation and counsel. That is, surely suggestions may be presented without the African side feeling "tricked." The mediator functions as an active leader of the procedure, and of the exposition of its content, all the way to the solution of the conflict. In the management of the conflict, i.e. in the "phase" of the presentation of the dispute, it is of special importance to begin by forming the plane of relations n such a way as to encourage the African side to "open its mouth". In many African ethnic groups there is a usage to the effect that a conflict may be spoken of, if at all, only when the relationship "clicks." There can therefore be no question of addressing conflicts substantially, directly, and uninterruptedly, but other viewpoints must preferably be brought under consideration, unless one wishes to reach the opposite of what is striven for.

It is not always the case that Africans' styles of communication manage a problem rectilinearly, or in a single trajectory. When the tread of a problem is dropped, Western mediators may expect that it will be taken up again later.

Under the premises of the intelligibility of t he choice of mediator, and the role of the mediator, it will now be in order to deal briefly with the compatibility of Western techniques of mediation (cf. chap. 3.4) with those of established Old African mediation. Western-oriented mediators here learn the "look" of the "toolbox" of techniques with which a European-African mediation can be successfully conducted.

Repeating the content and words of one of the parties to the conflict, that is, mirroring or reflecting this content and these words, is a culturally compatible technique for making sure of what a given party wishes to express. Furthermore, it is of interest for the other party to the conflict, since it enables it to hear from two sources what has been expressed.

The technique of active listening is of profound importance. Speaking and active listening may well be one of the great, astounding orientations of Southern Africa. It is here that oral culture demonstrates the power of living experience. It is not the written record of oral texts on the flip chart or bulletin board that is of importance here, but a reciprocal "hearkening", tone and feelings, the timber of the voice, bodily posture, what is meant in what is said indirectly.

Reframing is accorded its importance in intercultural mediation. This importance is greater first and foremost for the European party to the conflict. In Old African cultural orientations, to be sure, the expression of negative content, from the viewpoints that we have presented further above, is very difficult. Africans like to refer directly to their needs, and indicate their desires. Westerns, instead, attempt to rid themselves of their anger, their negative feelings and emotions. The technique of reframing, then, helps primarily the Europeans to come in contact with their needs, in intercultural mediation.

A favorite speech pattern in mediations in the Western cultural context consists in the call and the appeal, the application of the "I" form of address, in order to shed the "you" (sg.) recriminations! True, this technique of Western mediation is important for the Western side in the intercultural Western-African context. But the African side would interpret this speech rule otherwise, since what is important to the Africans is collective identity with their relational group—whether family, clan, nation, or peer group—and not a pointed expression of an individual kind.

The technique of doubling is definitely applied in certain situations. In the situation of mediation, the mediator stands momentarily on the side of the African party and speaks with its voice. This capacity, granted, is only manageable after extensive experience with African styles of doubling. Otherwise it is advised, to let the African counterpart practice this technique, in a tandem adopted on grounds presented above.

Africans are masterfully inculturated in non-violent confrontation (cf. chap. 3.5). When they make a statement about their own opinions, they often make use of positive formulations. Thereby they open the way for a pleasant culture of conversation. If one follows the valuable conceptualizations of Africans, worthy of their striving, then one sees in one's neighbor someone whom one empathetically accepts as s/he is—

with all of his/her faults and sensitivities. The European party need not regard itself as "shrouded over." Despair, grief, and gladness are emotional forms of non-violent communication, that, despite divergent cultural semantics, are open to being conveyed in the intercultural mediation process.

One technique that can be introduced simply and effectively lies in investigation (questioning) and concretization. It is not abstraction and general consideration that move the mediation process forward, but the experienced and describable situation. Of course, tabooed subjects are observable here, with which the technique of concretization cannot "normally" be applied.

The technique of praising has two sides. On the one side, it means "manipulating" one's neighbor toward higher achievement. On the other, praise can be related to a very concrete and describable situation, in which the one conflicting party has also enriched the other. In Old African contexts, praise serves for the optimization of social relations, but, of course, does not have the function of feedback to someone regarding her or his accomplishment.

The forming of syntheses genuinely corresponds to the cultural paradigms prevalent in Southern Africa. Separate analyses are obsolete, since the task is to connect individual elements and to develop communalities. Styles of thinking are holistic in African orientation, and can be harmoniously inserted into intercultural mediation.

In echoing, certain words of one of the conflicting parties are emphasized, in order to evoke their contradiction. This technique is to be applied with caution, since many Africans could perhaps feel themselves pushed into the background or even mimicked. The technique of active listening is needed throughout the area of intercultural mediation, since it is needed for conducting a conversation there in adequate fashion.

The technique of the paradoxical intervention is not advisable in Western-African mediation situations. Consisting of ironical interruption, it expects a reaction from the African party. But irony can only be understood by members of the same cultural relational group;

furthermore, as a rhetorical means of address it is foreign to most Africans. Thus, it is better to omit this technique. Painful situations could arise that would bring the course of the mediation to a halt

At the time, the technique of the switch of perspective has a very good chance of succeeding. Both conflicting parties wish to become acquainted with the viewpoint of the other, if they desire a mediation. A verbal repetition of the statements of the other party to the conflict must, of course, correspond to the feasibility of the proposition at hand.

With the technique of the formation of metaphors and analogies, we find ourselves on a "wide spectrum" of communication in processes of intercultural mediation. As has been detailed above, persons of Old African orientation prefer to speak indirectly, in images and comparisons, in idioms and analogies. This "hits on" what cannot be better expressed emotionally or in attitude. Metaphors clarify conflicts, at the same time as they supply images that contribute to the resolution of intercultural conflicts.

When hypotheses are proposed, it is presumed that irrealities are involved, or else scenarios that could be developed in future. Whether these attitudes find a correspondence on the African side can be doubted. This technique can be applied only in special situations of mediation.

The conjunction of sequential units of address broadens active listening, inasmuch as it is no longer only factual contexts, and feelings, that are reproduced, but also holistic combinations. This technique is very appropriate for bringing monochromic and polychromic management of confictive points to a new level, and thereby positively influencing the mediation process.

In many cultural contexts, it is surely meaningful to offer private conversations. It satisfies the need for explanation and information that, on certain grounds (taboos?), may not be supplied in the semi-public environment of a mediation session when strongly divergent cultural attitudes are a factor.

Owing to its Western "provenance", the technique of brainstorming is not to be introduced casually, as it aims too strongly at individual concerns. In a situation of intercultural mediation, it would be preferable to invoke a platform for counsel after the exemplar of Indaba and Shauri.

Africans have become particularly capable of perceiving and interpreting body language and its signs. They are experts in the art of reading relations, and the options these involve, from these, from movements, postures, distance and proximity of bodies. "Bodily semantics" is an area from which those involved in an intercultural situation, and, in particular, mediators, can "read out" possible solutions of the conflict under consideration.

A brief remark remains to be made with a view to techniques of inquiry. In order to realize a progress in the process of intercultural mediation, those involved ought not to be too stoutly confronted with closed questions. As for the technique of questioning, the need for harmony inclines many persons of African extraction to react positively to closed questions. Open questions, then, may open wider opportunities for the shaping of the mediation process.

Finally, if optimal results are to be obtained in Western-African intercultural mediations, a decisive factor is the framework and atmosphere that ought to be provided. First, florid Western aesthetics, with all of its less than straightforward messages, is not necessarily understood. Africans prefer the an enduring solution in the process of mediation. It must be recognizable by the African side what it receives in a solution, be it a gesture of invitation to a solemn affair, or be it a material compensation for injustice suffered—which, incidentally, is an exceedingly frequent solution in conflicts between Europeans and Africans.

It is a difficult venture when an attempt is made, in intercultural mediation, to verbalize the desire to be delivered from deeper needs that may be hidden behind the offences. There are at least two obstacles. First is the language barrier, second is the etiquette of African styles of communication. It is often difficult, even for bilingual speakers, to translate feelings and needs into accurate and appropriate semantics. Feelings defy translation. They are merely there, and seek their intuitive recognition and respect by the parties to the conflict—

frequently beyond linguistic competence and cultural etiquette. It is often the case that verbalizations of emotions and needs correspond to other sensations on the African side. For example, with many Africans, "astonishment" and, simply, "terror" constitute the only option for expressing emotions in the face of culturally incompatible behaviors on the part of the European party to the conflict. In the European understanding, annoyance, rage, anxiety, contempt, and disgust receive expression without any difficulty. But precisely these forms of expression would encounter the resistance and wonderment of the African side, as appearing most profoundly discourteous. For most Africans, linguistic expression has a magical function. From the African perspective, "bad language" may bring about precisely that which is to be avoided, namely, annoyance, discord, and disharmony. This seems to us to be an essential reason why Africans are so cautious in the choice of their words. Words work. They are not "sound and fury, signifying nothing."

Let us turn now to the goal striven for in a Western-African mediation. Different intercultural orientations manifest a large proportion of communalities. There is a large assortment of communalities in intercultural orientations. After all, it is of concern to both parties to be able to draw profit from the solution and to be content. It is an important aspect for Africans that respect for the individual/family/clan/nation be restored. Here we touch on a basic value, which constitutes the premise of human cohabitation, among one another, in the African image of the human being. Further, there follows the acknowledgment of rank and status that is striven for, those of the interests and positions of the conflicting parties. Depending on the location at which an intercultural mediation is found to be open to procedure, interest and positions will be less emphasized than, rather, the wish for further cooperation. To correspond to this wish, even interests and positions will, temporarily, be readily set aside. However, they remain as "conservative constants" in the conflict setting--further at hand, and effective over the long term.

The behavior of the conflicting parties should be kept in view. What role is played by the conflicting party that we find present in a person? Only in the rarest cases will the African side speak for itself alone. The "communitarian self" (cf.. chap. 5.5) is affected. Rather, what appear are formal statements of collective psychology. Every word has one's family of origin, dispatching institution, and spiritual security as a background. It is important that South Africans speak for themselves, inasmuch as, at the same time they are speaking for their personal cultural and "relational" group. When, for example, a female African student is not accommodated as her family of origin or ethnic origin would have expected for a guest, it may happen that she has the sensation of being discriminated against. This sensation will not be expressed before the hosts, however, but only when the student is back in her homeland. In this manner, the attitude of the group of origin is "enriched" by a collective foreign stereotype.

Argumentation is rather rarely conducted on the part of members of African culture. For them, heated argumentation is disturbing, since it can be an obstacle to listening and solution-finding. Besides, they prefer to express themselves in metaphors, sayings, and allegorical stories, because they know that the others involved in the mediation take more away from these than from "logical" argumentation.

It is abundantly clear to the African party to the conflict that it is not permitted to show any feelings and emotions, other than the emotions of joy and enthusiasm, sorrow and reflection. This behavior is intended to reflect its strength and self-control. The European side, on the other hand, may express feelings of anger, disgust, hatred, irritation, and offence. These seem to the European to correspond to authenticity and directness, but their effect on Africans is, instead, one of rejection and discourtesy, and in no way expresses interest, a quest for contact, or even engagement, in the eyes of the African side.

What purpose is served by the conflicting parties' linguistic communication? For the European side, speech is regarded as an instrument of information, a means of discussion, while the African side makes use of speech rather to dramatize, to unfold and develop "narrativity", or to transmit nonverbal gestures and demeanor. All of this against the background of speech in the sense of verbal communication having magical implications. By way of the word applied, a new reality is built, the word has effect, in good as in ill. For intercultural mediators, then, it is especially difficult to set these distinct patterns and styles of communication together, inn a synergic relation. As emerges from the research of comparative cultural science, the problem of "loss of face" is especially virulent in situations of conflict. For conflicting African parties, it is extremely difficult to yield to injustice. It is painful, shameful, and offensive to them. Such an act is possible only under special, constitutive conditions, as clarified above. Intercultural mediators are here required to guard the boundaries in a manner sensitive to culture, within which no loss of face be undergone by either of the parties to the conflict.

Finally, the subject of diverse cultural semantics is to be addressed. Avoidable misunderstandings in intercultural mediations lurk here.

First of all, the semantics—not the grammar—of the question is to be elucidated. In African conceptualizations, questions represent the fundamental schema of learning, and interests indicate the well-being of one's interlocutor. Whether at the first greeting, after a trip, or when you encounter an old friend, what is uppermost is not statements or imperatives, but: "How are you?" Therefore questions express participation and attention, which provide the single viable foundation for harmonious conversation in mediation. Questions, in the Old African sense, contain no irony according to Western understanding. Were irony applied by a Western party in a question, in intercultural mediation, it would be taken purely as a question about "real" existence, and by no manner of means recognized as humorous. It must be reformulated, and submitted to a reframing.

In escalation models of conflict situations, for the Western oriented mediator there is the appearance and potential of threat and menace. Working them out, and bringing them under control with appropriate techniques is also unconditionally necessary in intercultural mediation.

Threats, bursting forth verbally, are construed as a directly effecting reality in the perception of African parties, and are unconditionally to be eliminated from the mediation process.

The question of guilt and atonement, again, belongs neither to the form of Western-oriented mediation, nor to European-African mediation. In Africa, the decision on the guilt and atonement of those involved in the conflict is usually undertaken by institutional persons, while in Europe it is conducted by person-neutral institutions, such as courts. In European African mediation, the issue is rather the process that would lead to the restoral of relations. From the African viewpoint, the form of excuse or apology implies the petition for the reconstruction of the lost community, in the sense of accepted participation and membership. The semantics of excuse is called regret, and formal—not personal—acceptance if guilt. Oftentimes, in rituals of forgiveness or pardon, there is an emphasis on a compulsion by evil energies, or cooperation with some person capable of black magic. Responsibility for the formal act of forgiveness is therefore not adopted individually. The collective, or its spiritual representatives decide the adoption of the forgiveness, and the rite of pardon. For mediation in the intercultural context, this reciprocity of excuse and pardon, celebrated between the parties to the conflict is a decisive event for the resolution of conflicts.

Then, what about cultural gesture, and the mimicry of head-nodding, eye contact, laughing, and keeping silent? As is abundantly clear, in Southern Africa nodding is first and foremost communicative. Nodding the head implies that one is listening, and not that s/he is accepting obligation to what is now being said. Neither can it be concluded from head-shaking that "No" is the response. It may just as readily imply a possible—not necessary—rejection of what is being said. Alongside these semantics, however, nodding also signals agreement, and is usually accompanied by an affirmative verbal utterance. For intercultural mediation, this means that nodding is primarily to be interpreted as the contribution of a conflicting party that shows interest and participation in the existence of social contact in the mediation.

Eye contact is interpreted in extremely varying ways in Southern Africa. There are orientations of certain ethnic groups in which eye contact among certain family members is taboo on certain occasions. Frequently, eye contact for longer than "three seconds" is considered disrespectful, as it can be between elders and their juniors, or between persons of the different sexes. It is no sign of rebuff whatever, in situations of mediation, when the African party bows his/her head after the greeting, and avoids eye contact. Rather, it is a sign of respect, but ought not to be mistakenly taken as subordination, as it is frequently interpreted by persons of Western orientation.

For persons travelling in Southern Africa, the ebullience of many Africans is attractive, while laughing strikes them as strange--especially when it is perceived in connection with one's own uncertainty as to "how to behave. The numerous factors that generate laughing on the part of Africans are too complex to set forth here. Surely, in situations of unaccustomed intercultural meetings, and in the absence of script and schemata, one laughs. This laughing is a reflex, not, as Europeans often fancy, a "laughing–at," by someone assessing the encounter from an arrogant position. This observation also applies to situations of intercultural mediation, in the declarations and forms of presentation of the European party. It by no means implies a critical appraisal—which at times occurs, on the part of the Western progressive thinker, in the encounter between Europeans and Africans.

In conclusion, let us glance at the culturally so varied phenomenon of silence. From the Old African viewpoint, keeping silence can accompany wisdom, and counter the need or wish to express sore points in mediation. To speak would open wounds that have been inflicted, that would then, like a curse, come back constantly. Silence can mean courtesy, when social status, age, and position make it more advisable not to speak. Silence can mean assent, or it can signal most profound rejection, embitterment, or disappointment. Keeping silence can also represent grief, although grief is more usually connected with wailing, or singing and dancing. In the framework of intercultural mediation, silence means listening to one another, and using the opportunities to leave space between words, and so much talk, for the energies to gather that can create a synergistic solution.

6. Training Opportunities for the Acquisition of Mediation-Related Intercultural Competency

6.1 Acquisition of Intercultural Competencies

For mediators occupied in intercultural contexts and mediations, there are various ways to improve and broaden their intercultural competency, so that a secure entry into intercultural mediations becomes possible.

Intercultural training undertakings develop (or further develop) intercultural orientations, intercultural competencies, and intercultural consciousness. This occurs at the hands of trainers and mediators, who sketch out and conduct shorter or longer training programs specifically for the target groups. In these undertakings, a distinction is made between culture-specific training projects, which prepare persons for an encounter with persons of an altogether particular cultural origin, or culture-general operations, which transmit general intercultural competencies.

The concept, "intercultural competencies," includes, for example, the nonverbal communicative competency in an intercultural situation, the acquisition of language competencies, technical organizational skills with a view to other cultural systems, as well as the construction of intercultural and trans-cultural creativity, which means the development of new potentials for cooperation, and new goals, with a view to intercultural communication and encounter. The acquisition of intercultural competency includes furthermore intercultural orientation, and the development of an intercultural consciousness. By intercultural orientation, we understand (Flechsig 1996) "the appropriation of knowledge of general-cultural, culturally specific, and intercultural situations,... especially concepts and models of cultural theory, knowledge in foreign research. . . ." Further, these orientations include the construction or realistic appraisals bearing on persons of other cultural systems. The building of this last-named competency is closely connected with the construction of intercultural consciousness. After all, it includes a sensitivity to cultural differences, as well as, especially, to cultural communalities. Furthermore, it contains cultural self-experience, cultural self-reflection, and cultural self-awareness, which can be looked upon as starting points of intercultural broadening of competencies. Finally, we should like to cite one more point: that of dealing with cultural differences. Training programs that stress cultural differences and diversities are frequently combined under "Diversity Management Training." In the foreground, here, stands the learning of techniques and methods for dealing with experiences of cultural contrast, cultural conflicts, and one's own experience of culture shock. Here lies a special center of gravity in the interplay of affective, cognitive, and behavior-oriented competency-development. In other words, persons trained emotionally, mentally, and with regard to their own attitude, can focus on intercultural situations, and of course take charge of them.

Liebe (1996) observes that there are three very special levels on which an intercultural competency can be defined with a view to mediators.

- Knowledge and understanding of one's own shared culture
- Transformation of perspective
- Construction of a new culture

Accordingly, for the construction of a knowledge and understanding of the conflicting parties, mediators can assemble information on the culture, since, in order to act as a go-between, persons must have some indispensable knowledge and understanding of the cultural backgrounds of the conflicting parties. Such a culturally specific preparation gives mediators more certitude and awareness in dealing with persons of distinct cultural origin.

A further point along the route to the improvement of intercultural competency is the mediator's capacity to grasp the perspectives of the parties involved. Here, it is certain that no different (foreign) cultural perspective can be grasped otherwise than approximately, and only insofar as one can grasp a familiar one.

Now that we have seen which competencies are necessary, in order to act and "go between" in intercultural situations and mediations, we should like to indicate a route for the development of an intercultural personality, with the steps that are important for mediators. Immediately thereupon, we should like to present selected methods that are applied in intercultural trainings. In conclusion, we shall introduce a suggestion for an intercultural "mediation simulation" in the Western-African frame of reference.

6.2 The Development of an Intercultural Personality

If mediators now wish to form themselves further, with a view to their own intercultural competencies, it may be useful to confront the theoretical approaches to the development of intercultural competencies. We should like to present a model that offers the development stages of a personality from ethnocentrism to intercultural acculturation.

We must begin with the assumption that every person first faces the world with a basic attitude of ethnocentrism. In other words, each person first assumes that the culture that is his or hers is at the same time the best. One's own criteria of appraisal, then, are always oriented to the characteristic marks of one's own cultural provenance. Correspondingly, this human, "inborn" trait serves the development of a personally appropriated survival mechanism in the environment. By way of the development of intercultural competencies, persons become more able to transfer to other cultural systems, and adapt to foreign cultural environments. They can learn to accept other cultures, and no longer see their own culture as the ideal one, the one above all others.

Hoopes (1979) has worked out seven steps of intercultural development, through which a person passes on the way to the highest rung, which itself divides into four possibilities. It is a model that presents an idealized form of the intercultural personality.

```
Assimilation, acculturation, biculturalism, multiculturalism
                              ↑
                      Selective adoption
                              ↑
                     Appreciation/Valuing
                              ↑
                     Acceptance/Respect\
                              ↑
                        Understanding
                              ↑
                          Awareness
                              ↑
                        Ethnocentrism
```

Graph: Hoopes: Stages of Intercultural Personality

Development to the intercultural personality will be influenced, says Hoopes, through individual internal conditions and external (environmental) conditions, all of which have influence on the development of personality.

Individual external conditions	Intelligence, morality, intercultural experiences, linguistic development and knowledge of foreign languages, foreign and cultural scientific knowledge of one's own culture
External environmental conditions	Relations of power and authority, order of communication, national prejudices and stereotypes, opportunities for intercultural experiences, implicit cultural assumptions

At the base of the model stretches the rung of ethnocentrism, every person's point of departure: that which one learns from birth onward is to be affirmed and accepted. Thus, it is a matter of the fundamental rung or stage of personal survival, which simultaneously safeguards and protects one's own group. Once this step has been made, the step of awareness follows. Now the person notices that there are other cultural groups, groups that are "otherwise," and that possibly look "remarkable." Here, however, one does not consciously notice one's own culture. Then the next rung, that of understanding, is grasped the scene, when one notices another culture in a manner that is differentiated from the one that has prevailed until now, and takes cognizance of the fact that the confrontation with a culture is a complex process, that can be executed rationally. An emotional reaction, therefore, is replaced by rational understanding. The other culture, however, is still accounted "foreign" "strange," and "of a different kind," and is depreciated in contrast with one's own culture. Acceptance and respect begins when someone recognizes and acknowledges the validity of cultural differences. Here the acceptance of other cultures stands in the foreground, without having to be compared with one's own culture or judged in its light. Further, cultural aspects are accepted and respected that differ absolutely from one's own culture and can possibly generate negative emotions. Appreciation/Valuing vis-à-vis another culture appears when one recognizes the strengths and weaknesses of this culture, and one is in a position intentionally to appraise certain partial areas of the culture in question. A partial, selective adoption of attitudes or behaviors of other cultures can supervene when a person adjudges the new culture "good" or "desirable." The adoption of these selected aspects can occur through adaptation or appropriation, and can have the basis that a person can perhaps prefer to work better or more effectively in the new culture, or that he or she likes the newly won impressions better, or have a closer personal affinity with them.

At the top of the ladder stand the four "theoretical conditions" to be acquired. None of these conditions occurs in its pure form, as a separate condition or situation. These four conditions or situations can be seen as "directions" in which persons can move, when they have attained to an advanced rung in intercultural learning. However, the signposts on the seventh rung are flexible and alterable, and not firmly defined.

Under assimilation/acculturation is understood a person's taking and adopting behaviors in a new cultural context, but without surrendering the first acculturation of the old cultural context. Adaptation takes place when a person can behave and move in a new cultural context appropriately and successfully. One speaks of biculturalism when a person possesses a twofold cultural identity, and can summon up and introduce both cultural identities, as needed. Finally, multiculturalism means that intercultural awareness, and intercultural competencies as generalized capabilities, are at hand. These capabilities then secure it that a person can adapt to, and freely move in, each new cultural context, in a relatively brief time, and without fear of disorientation.

Personal confrontation with this model can serve one's own cultural self-reflection, and bring consciousness into one's own manners of acting, thinking, feeling, and moving, in a new intercultural situation. Here we suggest that one not see the model so "step-wise" as it is sketched. In practice, it becomes clear very soon that the transitions between the rungs are not always clearly divided, and that the boundaries blend into one another. Besides, the surprising phenomenon may be observed, that, with regard to one culture, one is on the sixth step, while with regard to another culture one has only reached the third. The model can therefore be introduced either in a manner specific to a given culture, or in a manner transcending it, and always needs a concrete thematic relation.

For us, this model is intended simply to map the trajectory of a possible way of development to the intercultural personality, in order to generate awareness capable of the construction of one's own intercultural personality, of which, as mediators, we have a need in intercultural contexts.

Unfortunately, we cannot present the different theoretical approaches and models one by one. In this connection, we recommend, for further reading, Krewer's (1994) "Vier-Stufen-Modell interkultureller Persönlichkeitsentwicklung" ("Four-Step Model of Intercultural Personality Development"), and Bennett's (1998) DMIS Model (Developmental Model of Intercultural Sensitivity).

6.3 Methods of the Acquisition of Intercultural Competency

Having now seen that everyone can acquire intercultural competencies, and direct his or her personality toward this aspect, the questions arise: what methodological and technological opportunities are there in the area of intercultural training for working on the development of intercultural competencies? And how can mediators actually school themselves, in order to improve intercultural competencies? Which culture-specific or intercultural learning styles need to be acknowledged?

In the following section, we should like briefly to present certain selected methods that seem particularly important to us in respect of the broadening of the cognitive, affective, and behavioral aspects of our own personality - and this with a view to intercultural contexts - and that invite a more profound acquaintance by interested persons.

The methods that we propose to present on the coming pages are applied to this form in culture-transcending, rather than in culture-specific, trainings. Examples are given for the following methods of intercultural training:

- Confrontation with theoretical models, theories of culture, and culture orientations (as, e.g., the model of the intercultural personality according to Hoopes, the iceberg-model of culture, the concept of culture according to Hofstede, etc.)
- Cultural self-experience
- Cultural other-experience
- Case studies
- Culture-assimilators (CA)
- Alienation exercises
- Simulations and role-playing

In addition to methods of culture-general training, culturally specific trainings often contain the following aspects, which we shall not further investigate in this book.

- Confrontation with culturally specific phenomena and cultural orientations of the country / the culture
- Problems of country and country-scientific orientation
- Language instruction
- The learning of opportunities and rules for behavior
- The decoding of manners and rules of behavior

If we have a closer look at these methods it is obviously that we need to connect them to learning styles. Individual learning styles, thoughts and feelings are very much connected to culture and culture-specific types of learning as well as to the defined roles of learner and a trainer or teacher, that means to the definition of social relationships in a society.

We can differentiate for basic types of learning which we can also find in intercultural settings (according to Kolb (1984)/ Barmeyer (2000:327):

Learning through:

- concrete experience
- reflection, perception and observation
- abstract cognition and conceptualization
- active experiments

If we want to train intercultural competence we need to adjust our training concept to the different learning styles of the participants. Therefore it is helpful to connect learning styles to training methods as follows:

Learning Styles & Training Methods

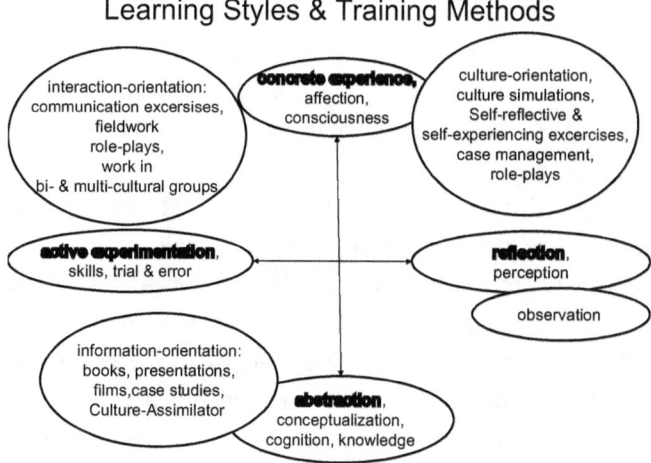

Graph: Learning Styles and Training Methods

6.4 Cultural Self-Experiencing and Experience of Cultural Alienation

Cultural self-experience can be attained through various methodological approaches. Individuals and groups can conduct exercises in self-experience vis-à-vis their own culture through methods such as, for example, self-interrogation, and a subsequent self-analysis, in terms of cultural phenomena, or in terms of one's own cultural identity. Theoretical reflections on the cultural orientations of the different socio-cultural groups, to which we belong, usually accompany such exercises in self-reflection. Further, theoretical models of culture are frequently introduced, in order to set these in connection with one's own experiences.

Furthermore, simulated experiences in cultural contrast are oftentimes built into the process of self-reflection in the form of role-playing or simulation. If the participants have already had many real experiences of cultural contrast, then the latter can be addressed, and developed analytically.

Manners of methodological procedure that play a role in the development of cultural self-experience, and in self-perception are: first, the thematization of the experienced and contacted self; second, the "structuration" of the self-experience and the self-perception; third, the problematization of that which has been experienced; fourth, the discussion of that which has been experienced; and finally, fifth, the confrontation with the self and with other opportunities for perception, expression, intention, interpretation, and appraisal, that are to be found outside one's own self.

Often, attached to the conduct of simulations or real culture-contrast experiences, are confrontation with one's own cultural schemata for self-reflection (cf. chap. 6.7), as well as culturally different opportunities for interpretation and appraisal.

The method of cultural experience of the other can, as already mentioned, be grasped and develop through the experience of simulated foreign cultural or real foreign cultural phenomena. Often, persons in everyday situations are not conscious of reflection on one's own self by way of their own cultural pattern. In most cases, processes of self-experience occur first after collision with experiences of foreign culture. If, for instance, Westerns in Africa notice that men often hold hands when strolling and talking, that will probably be striking from a Western's cultural viewpoint. Probably it will evoke a cultural schema of homosexual men, whom they have often seen behaving in this way in large Western cities. Now they will consider whether the number of homosexual men in Southern Africa is substantially higher than it is in Germany. If they find themselves for prolonged periods in Sub-Saharan contexts, surely they will eventually have to store a new cultural schema of "men holding hands." After all: in African contexts, men hold hands in order to assure their friendship, and to shape personal relations in a positive and trusting manner.

In this fashion, the experience of foreign culture necessarily leads from culturally specific semantics to a reflection on one's own cultural context, and, desirably, to the "relativization" of one's own cultural inventory. Finally, one hopes, it will lead to the culturally adequate interpretation of a behavioral repertoire usual in many of the cultures of Africa.

6.5 Case Studies

Case studies offer learners a situation in a complex form, in which various cultural standards and cultural orientations become typological concrete. It is the task of the learners to analyse the situation, to "distil out" the cultural orientations, to undertake changes in perspective and, in given instances, to discuss suggestions for a solution.

Case studies differ from "critical events" inasmuch as, while they do also present typified situations, the situations are directed only upon one culturally foreign focus, and renounce complex behavioral connections. Case studies can contain uni-perspective or pluri-perspective cases. As further variants for a case history, the method of reciprocal perspective is available. The construction of the pluri-perspective leads to, for instance, tasks that contain the formation of hypotheses, as the image of one's own culture is presented in a person's head from the foreign culture.

Furthermore, the structure of case studies varies. The formulation of the cases can represent either a closed or an open form. The closed form is more of an analytical challenge as a consequence. On the other hand, an open case has a creative development as its consequence, in the sense of the further description of a case, or a confrontation with the varying perspectives.

The following case study (see also Mayer, C.-H., Boness, C., Thomas, A. (2003)) is intended to illustrate how an open pluri-perspective case history can look, and what questions are to be attached to it.

A Case Study

In the Tanga district of North-Eastern Tanzania, in the coastal area, an internationally sponsored environmental program is in progress. It is set up in collaboration with the local diocese, and is open to those interested. A Monday-to-Friday seminar program, on the village level, forms the core of the project, and is intended to inform participants on the problems of "desertification." At the same time, it is intended to motivate the small farmers involved to undertake activities themselves, for the betterment of the soil. The first three days of the seminar are devoted to introducing persons into the basic set of problems, while on the last two days a model tree-school is erected. A good twenty persons participate, and work with interest. On the third day of the seminar, however, during her lecture on "forestation and erosion control," the Western forester notices that the participants no longer listen so intently, but are occupying themselves with other things instead. The following day, work is to begin on the model tree school, but the expected cooperation does not occur. The European expert is irritated: the practical part of the seminar is threatening to fail. Finally, on the last day of the seminar, the Western had to observe that the number of participants has sunken to eight. As the bishop present notices the insecurity of the Western forest expert, he goes to the front of the room and holds an address, in which he appeals to the participants to cooperate in the preservation of God's creation. And so at least a part of the model tree school is saved.

Shortly before the official end of the environmental seminar, the bishop privately asks the forester to give the participants some money for their good work.

Sample Questions on the Case

- What do the Tanzanian participants likely think of the Western expert?
- What do the Tanzanian participants likely think of their own behavior?
- What does the Western expert likely thin of the Tanzanian participants?
- What does the Western expert think of her own role?

6.4 Culture Assimilators

At this point we should like to present an additional training method, one that is repeatedly introduced for general as well as culturally specific "sensitisation." True, in recent years the culturally specific culture assimilators become familiar. A basis for this may lie in the fact that learners wish to prepare themselves for specific regions of this world to which they are to travel.

Frequently, in the Anglophone literature, accounts of situations of critical encounters are re-formed into a culture assimilator. On grounds of connotation, the Anglophone literature also likes to call CA the "intercultural sensitizer" (Albert 1995, p. 157). This method of intercultural training is introduced for sensitisation vis-à-vis manners of behavior, norms, perceptions, attitudes values, and interpretations, in intersecting cultural situations.

Originally, this method served for the improvement of communication in intercultural labor groups. Today it is further introduced especially in respect of intercultural training goals. Its main communality with the method of critical events (cf. cap. 6.5) consists in the fact that both training methods are attained on the basis of a particular choice of converted "critical incidents." These lead through a set of questions for development, with a subsequent feedback phase, to a preponderantly cognitive learning achievement through phenomena of one's own and the foreign culture. While the method of critical events is indebted more to the pedagogical concept of "experimental" learning, the questions to be developed in the CA rely rather on the basic assumptions of "programmed learning."

The conduct of the CA method consists of the following procedural manners. A critical incident is described. Subsequently to the situation presented, there follow one or more questions concerning the behavior, thoughts, or feelings of a person described. As a rule, three to five interpretational alternatives are formulated, of which the reader/participant is to select the most probable answer, and the others their relative correctness, in order. For the empirical development of the interpretational alternatives, members of the target culture, as well as members of the applying culture, are subjected to questioning. The distillation of these questions consists partly of very numerous variants of explanation, finally from gradually rejected attribution alternatives, which all have a minimum degree of correctness. One of the three to five alternatives proposed for answers, however, is most correct. The other interpretational alternatives have a lesser degree of correctness, in the sense of "isomorphic attribution." As a rule, three to five alternative interpretations are formulated, of which the reader/participant selects the most probable response, while the others estimate the respective degree of correctness in them all. For the empirical development of the alternative interpretations, both the members of the target culture, and those of the culture of application, are questioned. The distillation of this of this somewhat numerous varying answers consists ultimate of gradually "filed" alternatives of attribution is most appropriate, however. The other interpretational alternatives enjoy a lower degree of correctness sin the sense of "isomorphic attribution."

Subsequently to consideration of the attribution alternatives, the learners are given a feedback, that presents and elucidates the possibilities of interpretation according to their probability. Each participant can individually appraise his or her particular competency in view of awareness, sensitivity, and the opportunity for a switch in perspective, and go through the situation once more with the newly acquired knowledge. CA is usually ordered to methods of cognitive learning: here lies the center of gravity on the transmission of information,, although, in a certain measure, the experimental learning is addressed through "trial and error," as also the behavior-oriented learning by way of the introduction of feedback.

Here we should like to illustrate the Culture Assimalator with an example from Southern Africa (see also Mayer, C.-H., Boness, C., Thomas, A. (2004)).

Rituals in Everyday Work

In Mpumalanga, Mr. Sotho maintains a warehouse for household utensils produced from recycled materials. A Western businessman, Mr. Knobloch, is interested in this segment of the regional trade sector,, and would like to enter into a collaboration. To this end, he seeks out Mr. Sotho's office. He is greeted, and is immediately offered a place by Mr. Sotho. Mr. Knobloch looks around the office a bit, and his gaze rests on a flat skin, in which several, apparently eaten, bird skeletons are to be seen, with sinews and gristle, immediately before him on the office desk. Disgust runs through the Western businessman, and he can scarcely continue to concentrate on the conversation. For this reason, finally, he asks Mr. Sotho to kindly have the leavings of the day before removed. Mr. Sotho is slightly irritated; however, he simply places the skin on the window sill behind him. The conversational atmosphere seems disturbed. Finally Mr. Sotho asks the Western to drop in again the next week.

Why does Mr. Sotho adjourn the conversation?

Read through all of the alternative explanations, and rank them on the following scale.

A. Direct requests do not correspond to the South African style of communication.

|⎿──────────────|───────────────|───────────────|──────────────⏌|

    Most likely   Fairly likely   Fairly unlikely   Least likely

B. Mr. Sotho is irritated that Mr. Knobloch doesn't see any sense in sacrificial gifts. Therefore he breaks off the meeting.

|⎿──────────────|───────────────|───────────────|──────────────⏌|

    Most likely   Fairly likely   Fairly unlikely   Least likely

C. Mr. Sotho is irritated because he understands Mr. Knobloch's request as a criticism. He feels offended, and so breaks off the discussion.

|⎿──────────────|───────────────|───────────────|──────────────⏌|

    Most likely   Fairly likely   Fairly unlikely   Least likely

Feedback on the alternative explanations

A. True, in large parts of Southern Africa, especially among Bantuethnic groups, indirect styles of communication prevail. Thus, it is generally expected of Western merchants that they make use of that kind of style when they carry on conversations with their partners. In Southern Africa, in recent years, this style of communication has been more and more changed among members of Bantu ethnic groups. Along with the indirect style of communication, in contact with other Southern African populations, a rather direct style of communication has developed, in which requests may be expressed politely and relative directly. With members of Western origin, as well as with those who belong to the „coloured" population groups, the direct style of communication, in comparison with that of Bantu ethnic groups, has always been rather direct. In the urban economic centers of Southern Africa, the conduct of a conversation tends, withhal, to be of a Western tone, and thereby more direct than in conversations conducted in Old African. Even if the kind of direct request were to be unpleasant for Mr. Sotho, he would presumably not break off an important business conversation because of it. Many Southern Africans know that Western-oriented persons have interiorised such a style. The alternative answer, besides, is formulated very generally, and is not conducive to the goal.

B. It is easily understandable that Mr. Knobloch should express the wish to have the dish with the presumed remains removed, since, to him, such a situation does not seem appropriate for a serious business conversation. Granted, Mr. Knobloch has missed the fact that Mr. Sotho ascribes the dish a completely different meaning and importance. Many members of Bantu ethnic groups cultivate a close magical relation to their ancestors and spirits. It is they who intervene in the life of the families, determine success and failure, influence all possible projects positively or negatively, and bring harmony into human relationships. To Mr. Sotho, then it is very important that, in his business area, even on the writing desk in his office, a sacrificial gift for his family ancestors always stand prepared. There can also be gifts that are there simply to appease menacing spirits or powers.

When we know this background, it is easy to understand that Mr. Sotho should be irritated by Mr. Knobloch's reaction. He would not care to engage in business relations with a partner who neither knows that it is sacrificial gifts here, nor accords them any interest and respect. Naturally, Mr. Sotho is also afraid that such a business partner could rile the ancestors and spirits, and could occasion harm for the business or the family. That is why Mr. Sotho decides to renounce the business, and such a business partner. And so the conversation is adjourned.

C. It is altogether possible that Mr. Knobloch's erequest for intervention be felt as completely inappropriate. It would be hard to find a businessman that would allow himself t be addressed by another, unknown businessman, how he must arrange and shape his office. Such a request would really be apprehended as a censure, then: with many Bantu ethnic groups it would be taken as a personal criticism, and be classified as very impolite. Persons and things are not experienced as separated, and it can well be that Mr. Sotho feels insulted here. However, this is not absolutely determinative for the abrupt ending of the conversation.

6.7 Exercises in Alienation

Besides the methods so far presented, alienation exercises are also introduced as methods of training. In all probability, alienation exercises are conducted rather at the beginning of training sequences, in order to evoke attention, reflection, and curiosity. Subsequently to such exercises, in situations of cultural intersection, affective and cognitive experiences of learners are readily appended.

One type of simple alienation exercise consists in, for example, that the contexts of the action are known, while the activity being performed in this context originates in foreign contexts. This renders obsolete the meaning of the action in the concrete context. A more complex type of alienation exercise consists in the context and actions being unknown in the same manner. Now the challenges to the learner are essentially more complex. Thus, there are various levels of complexity in the alienation exercises, the degree of complexity correlating with the higher requirements in learners' affective and cognitive capabilities.

Here we present an easy example of an alienation exercise of medium complexity: Martian Anthropology (see also Flechsig (2001) and Kohls/Knight (1994)).

Martian Anthropology

Scenario

In this exercise, you are to take on the role of inhabitants of Mars, who are sent to earth as ethnologists, to study the culture there. Your assignment is to conduct a research operation, but—without knowing it-- you get into a "false" setting, in the Western cultural context. There you initiate observations, which you interpret with your "cultural script."

Example: You come upon a bowling alley, and, after consulting your assignment sheet, interpret everything you see in terms of religious practice.

Research Assignment

You select an investigative assignment from your assignment list, and then look (mentally) for the place indicated for observation. There you interpret the lifestyle, activities, and social structure in terms of the inquiry presented in the assignment. The purpose of your report will later be to prepare a delegation of important Martian politicians for your communication with terrestrials.

Execution

You have twenty minutes to write brief notes for an investigative report. Each team of anthropologists now takes a report to the entire body of scientists, to report their experiences on earth. The reports are to serve in the preparation of a delegation of Martian politicians for negotiations with the terrestrials.

Assignment list:

Go to/Into: **and there study:**

Shop   *Justice and legal system*

Supermarket   *Arming/food supply/harvest*

Bookstore   *Medical practice / health system*

McDonalds   *Family life*

Bank   *Educational system*

Pub/Café   *Politics/administration/government*

Sanitorium   *Military/defense*

City library   *Use of free time*

Hospital   *Arts/art works/art expressions*

Post office   *Social organization*

Laundary   *Science and technology*

Bowling alley   *Religious practice*

Evaluation of the Martian Anthropology

For an evaluation of the exercise, we should like to make some suggestions for possible lines of questioning

- How did your exercise „go"? How did you feel?
- Were there things that struck you as especially easy?
- Were their difficulties? If yes, which?
- What was your mental attitude during this exercise?
- What perspective did you adopt for the perception and interpretation of the environment?
- Have you an idea of why such a change in perception is so difficult?
- Do you know such phenomena from your own daily life?
- When do you meet with such phenomena from your daily life?
- Is there a relation to situations of intercultural encounter?
- If yes, then what does this relation look like?
- What happens when you find yourself in a situation in a culture foreign to you?
- What have you brought personally to the alienation exercise?

Conclusion: A Brief Look at the Schema Theory

One's own framework of relations is the basis of all of one's own perceptions, expressions, interpretations, intentions, and evaluations. This framework of relations is marked culturally and individually.

From birth onward, every human being has stored certain schemata, certain situations and experiences (cf. chap. 6.4). Thus, schemata are a kind of help for everyday orientation,, perception, and activity. They perform various functions. On one hand, the stored schemata should be "correctly" perceived, understood, interpreted, and evaluated. At the same time, they should function as a help for behavioral sureness in complex everyday situations. Further functions of the schemata are the storing and memory-recall of what has been experienced and learned, as well as the connection of certain associated elements of different schemata. Through the schemata, everyday activities can be automatized and quickly conducted. Activity is regulated by the brain itself. Persons are unburdened, inasmuch as they no longer need to reflect on the smallest acts undertaken in complex situations.

The formation of schemata passes, for example, by way of cognitive learning processes, affective experience and experience of events, and the exercise of activities and (new) behavioral variants. Schemata can be stored, revised, and broadened lifelong.

For intercultural experiences, the approach to theory of schemata means that, especially in new cultural surroundings, new schemata must be repeatedly formed, and old ones restructured. Here there can be no reference to already established schemata, since these are culturally incompatible with the new situation. In many cases, the application of culturally incompatible schemata leads to experiences of culture shock, leading to alterations in the applied schemata.

Alienation exercises - in proportion to their degree of complexity - serve to render one's schemata conscious, restructured, to broaden them, or to construct them altogether anew.

6.8 Simulations and Role-Playing

Role playing and simulations are performed on various levels of design and execution. Simulations introduced into intercultural trainings evince a particular structure, in which the following factors are operative.[1]

First, it is important to describe a context in which the simulation is to take place. Then, roles are divided among actors, who develop their role descriptions, in order then to be able to perform them concretely. These role descriptions can seem very simple, but they also set the players high challenges. As a rule, scripts contain particular traits, attitudes, behaviors, and value orientations of a person In addition, there are indications of ways of behavior, and invitations to action, that can be concretely applied to the role playing or the situation. Thus, expression bound to value-orientation can become visible in the role-playing, on the level of action and behavior.

Frequently, particular resources are introduced that are helpful in embodying the role externally.

Role playing and simulations vary in time, number of persons, and the formation of content. For intercultural simulations: content, like action in intercultural contexts, multicultural counselling, conflicts over attitudes toward work, management of time, or dealing with property, are all available.

When the role playing or simulations are over, trainers should ritually or formally discharge the players from their roles, and return to their daily personalities. A group appraisal follows.

They are now introduced into an intercultural situation of simulation, that, depending on experience, are drawn into in mediation formation, since they are especially suited for the schooling and sensitising of continuing mediators in view of contexts of intercultural mediation, as well. It suggests itself that the simulation in intercultural trainings be introduced to Southern Africa, or for preparation for Western-African interaction.

6.9 A Western-African Mediation Simulation
A Conflict among Colleagues
Schedule and Course of the Simulation for Trainers

Time frame: ca. 2-5 hours

Phase 1: Formation of small groups, distribution of work assignments

- A mediation team, consisting of two mediators
- A role-player: Ms. Schmidt
- A role-player: Ms. Mugalo

The roles can be played by men and women. A skirt is recommended for both women (or, when men play the part, a coat)

- Observers

Observers receive no job slips; however, they should attend to the following points.

- Where do culture and cultural orientations occupy the foreground?
- What cultural orientations area at play, on the side of Ms. Schmidt and Ms. Mugalo?
- At what places in the process do (female) gender roles enter the foreground?

Phase 2: Preparation in small groups

- The preparation is done in small groups: persons with the same role descriptions or work assignments (e.g., both Ms. Schmidt's, both Ms. Mugalo's, all observers, and the mediators) meet for their common preparation.
- Ca. 15 minutes

Phase 3: Mediation Role Playing

- Playing of the mediation role in small groups
- Ca. 45-60 minutes

Phase 4: Small-group discussion

- Discharge of the role-players from their roles
- Observations and statements by the mediators and role players
- Remarks of the observers
- Ca. 30 minutes

Phase 5: Presentation of the work-results and discussion in the forum
- Ca. 30-45 minutes, as needed

A Conflict among Colleagues" Information for the Mediators[1]

General Information

Ms. Schmidt and Ms. Mugalo have been working together for some months on the same team of the "Verein für integrative Jugendhilfe und gesellschaftliche Eingliederung, e.V." ("Union for Integrative Youth Assistance and Social Incorporation"), in Frankfurt am Main, Germany. The team is comprised of six persons, and is composed multi-culturally. Ms. Schmidt is Western, Ms. Mugalo is Kenyan by birth, but has lived in Germany for fifteen years. The other members of the team are an Iranian, a Russian, a Turk, and a Brazilian. The concept of the Union is structured so that two persons always work, together and intensively, on one project. A project has corresponding regional cultural work centers of gravity. Thus, Ms. Schmidt's and Ms. Mugalo's project cares for the "integration of African youth between the ages of twelve and eighteen in the Western public school.

Ms. Schmidt has worked in the Union for fifteen years, and loves her work above all else. For seven years, she has worked mainly with Africans, and, as she herself says, gets along especially good with this target group.

Ms. Mugalo has been active in the Union, as a new team member, only six months. She previously worked in a youth establishment for unaccompanied minor refugees, mainly coming from Eastern Europe. She applied for the position because she wished to work with African youth. Last but not least, she feels that she can contribute strong biographical competencies

For some four months, now, confrontations have repeatedly arisen between Ms. Schmidt and Ms. Mugalo. The problems have been discussed in a team setting, and with supervisors, but disagreements appear: relative to work area, acknowledgment of each other's competencies, management of work and time. Seemingly, it is always just a matter of "details." However, morale on the team has sunken to the point that it already seems to make itself noticeable and visible in the lower quality, and effectiveness, of work. Team members have also generally "called in sick" more often in the past four months.

After the last discussion, a team member suggests that, after all, the conflicting parties could have a mediation session conducted. Ms. Schmidt and Ms. Mugalo both agree to have a mediation to solve the problems.

After the introductory team discussions with both parties have become private ones, Ms. Schmidt and Ms. Mugalo come to their first joint mediation session today.

A Conflict between Colleagues: Role Desciption - Ms. Mugalo

Ms. Mugalo is forty-seven years of age, and has been living in Germany for fifteen years. She is a Kenyan by birth, married to a Western husband, and has three children, with whom she likes to spend her free time.

Argumentation und Background

Every morning, when she comes to the office, Ms. Mugalo greets each team member individually, and with a bit of small talk." By the time she gets to her desk, thirty minutes of her work time have already gone by. The morning greeting has a very high value for her: in her opinion, it furthers a good atmosphere on the team, and thereby a good common, fore effective collaboration.

When Ms. Mugalo thinks she has done her work, she goes home, without looking for any extra work, or discussing this with Ms. Schmidt. She does not work extra hours. Sometimes, however, without discussing it with Ms. Schmidt, she works of projects longer, or takes them on, too do her a favour. She is very puzzled that Mrs. Schmidt never responds in kind, and take work from her without request or appeal. Ms. Mugalo's favors are always taken amiss, without this ever having to be mentioned explicitly. Meanwhile, Ms. Mugalo is very anger, and feels that Ms. Schmidt does not respect her.

Even when Ms. Mugalo tries to present African views and values to Mrs. Schmidt, or to suggest them, she feels rejected, since Ms. Schmidt does not seem interested in her explanation. At any rate, she does not say anything about it.

Ms. Mugalo likes to work at her own speed, divides her time on her own schedule, and usually works on several projects at once. For her, this way of working is stimulating, and creative, and substantially more motivating than working on one project at a time until it is finished. One result of this work style is that it is often weeks before Ms. Mugalo's final work reports are turned in, which seems to irritate Ms. Schmidt. At the end of the month, then, she submits several reports at one time, which Mrs. Schmidt has to "clear" before she can lead her on to the higher position. Ms. Mugalo finds this way of working very productive and intensive, and can then submit several projects at the end of one of one project phase. She simply cannot understand why Ms. Schmidt is constantly complaining that Ms. Mugalo cannot develop her own type of intense attention to her work.

While she works, Ms. Mugalo likes to talk about her family, and is also very interested in Ms. Schmidt's family life, to make a nice atmosphere, as well as to make a nice indication of her interest in her colleague. She is repeatedly taken aback that Ms. Schmidt is so reticent, and that she does not like to expose anything about herself and her family. Ms. Mugalo thinks that this is being uncommunicative, and thinks that Ms. Schmidt has certainly something to hide and is to be handled with care.

She does not like to address problems that come up with Ms. Schmidt directly, and constantly expresses herself in such a way that harmony and mutual agreement can be ultimately restored after a disagreement. Besides, she finds it extremely undisciplined that Ms. Schmidt makes her complaints directly to her. When Ms. Schmidt confronts her verbally, she is very taciturn and reticent. If Ms. Mugalo ever reacts to the confrontation at all, then she turns to another team member and presents the latter with her view of things.

When possible, Ms. Mugalo avoids length eye contact with anyone, as she feels this is to show disrespect to her conversational partner.

A Conflict between Colleagues: Role Description - Ms. Schmidt

Ms. Schmidt is fifty-six years old, and has worked for fifteen years for the same "boss." She is married, and has a daughter, who has long since left home. Since then, Ms. Schmidt lives solely for her job, which she finds very enjoyable.

Argumentation and Background

Ms, Schmidt lives for her work. She is very punctual, greets her colleagues only briefly and tersely, and devotes herself as soon as possible to her daily tasks. Ms, Schmidt is very orderly, and exactly "into what she's doing." She works continuously and rapidly. It "gets on her nerves" very much that Ms. Mugalo greets the colleagues verbosely,, and so shortens her work time.

Ms. Schmidt frequently remains in the office, in order to do preparation work for the next day. It is usually the case that she works through one project per week, from start to finish, and completes her project with a report then given to her colleague Mugalo to read through after it has been finished. It annoys her whenever the report lies on Ms. Mugalo's desk for days, delaying the project's final report, because Ms. Mugalo works on several projects at once.

Nor can she at all understand that, instead of finishing a project at the same time as she does, Ms. Mugalo prefers to work on four projects at once for four weeks, and then finishes them all at once at the end of the month. It especially disturbs her that she must then edit all four projects at once, which means "piles of work," and usually involuntary additional hours on the last day of the month.

If Ms. Mugalo goes to Ms. Schmidt's desk to take over some projects without asking, or to continue the latter's work on them, for her this is interference in her work area, which she feels as disrespectful. Often, in recent weeks, Ms. Mugalo has tried to reconcile Ms. Schmidt on this point, but Ms. Schmidt seems not to undertake any alterations in her *modus procedendi*.

Ms. Schmidt likes to separate her private life from her work, and does not like to talk with colleagues about her private and family life. All the more is she irritated that Ms. Mugalo repeatedly asks about her family and their personal lifestyles. Rather, she finds that her colleague is invading private territory, it is simply none of her business, and besides, it eats up precious work time.

Ms. Schmidt likes to address disagreements directly, without beating around the bush, inn order to clarify the situation at once and give vent too her dissatisfaction. She always becomes more irate when Ms. Mugalo reacts reticently and indirectly to her assertions, and "without once looking her iin the face." It provokes her a great deal when she then hears from other team members that Ms. Mugalo only speaks with them about her view, instead of turning directly to Ms. Schmidt.

In addition, Ms. Schmidt finds it very humiliating that Ms. Mugalo always hints at African viewpoints to Ms. Schmidt. Ms. Schmidt thinks that, after all these years of professional experience, she still does not have enough intercultural competency to introduce the integration of African youth herself, and in her own way!

Having presented, in various examples, selected training opportunities for the acquisition of intercultural competencies related to mediation, let us look at the opportunities for an innovative application of intercultural mediation and the working out of conflicts.

7. Prospect

The intent of this book is to present to the interested public a new, partial segment of intercultural mediation. It contains the spectrum of theoretical foundations of the subject, building blocks for implementation, and, along with numerous indications and suggestions, a focus on the regional culture of Southern Africa. Interested readers can "read up a competency" with this book, in order to be "armed" for a management of the ever growing number of situations of conflict in intercultural contexts.

The building blocks of Western-African realities can be introduced in the most diverse areas. First, it would be in order to introduce this work in connection with the formation of mediators, since we present the goal, additional intercultural qualifications, in this association. Next, the book provides trained and long-experienced mediators with information and factual knowledge in an area, that, in future, will gain in relevance for the practice of their vocation. It is also intended as a help for instructors in mediation, and intercultural trainers, who approach this area as an opportunity for their own program of schooling, if they wish to acquire an insight into the respective unfamiliar areas.

Autodidact managers, professional and leadership authorities, will scarcely be able to do without such a book, in view of both the composition of their intercultural teams, and their intercultural personnel management. Especially, this book can make an effective contribution to Western-African leadership in negotiation, since it is especially based on research, information, and long years of experience, with persons of Southern Africa.

Since it presents more than a trend in the area of publications on intercultural mediation, this book, the readership may be assured, can introduce meaningful improvement in their competency, both in their professional life, and in their private everyday one.

8. Literatur

Adam, H. und Moodley, K. (1993):
The Opening of the Apartheid Mind - Options for the New Democratic South Africa. Berkley University Press.

Allport, G. (1954):
The nature of prejudice. Macmillian, New York.

Anderson, B. (1983):
Die Erfindung der Nation. Zur Karriere eines erfolgreichen Konzepts. Propyläen Taschenbuch. Aus dem Englischen „Imagined Communities" von Benedikt Burkhars und Christoph Münz. Erweiterete Ausgabe. Berlin:Ullstein.

Augsburger, D.W. (1992):
Conflict Mediation Across Cultures. Kentucky: John Knox Press.

Avruch, K. (1998):
Culture and Conflict Resolution. USIP Press, Washington D.C.

Bennett, M. (1995):
Critical Incidents in an Intercultural Conflict-Rsolution Exercise. In: Fowler, S.M. & Mumford, M.G.: Intercultural Sourcebook: Cross-cultural Training Methods. Vol.1, Yarmouth. Intercultural Press, S. 147-156.

Bennett, M. (1998):
Intercultural Communication: A Current Perspective. In: Bennett, M. (Hrsg.): Basic Cooncepts of Intercultural Comunication, Yarmouth, Maine 1998, S. 26ff.

Berger, P.L. / Luckmann, T. (1977):
Die gesellschaftliche Konstrukton der Wirklichkeit. Eine Theorie der Wissenssoziologie. 17. Auflage. Fischer Verlag, Frankfurt a.M..

Berger, P.L. / Luckmann, T. (2000):
Die gesellschaftliche Konstrukton der Wirklichkeit. Eine Theorie der Wissenssoziologie. 17. Auflage. Fischer Verlag, Frankfurt a.M..

Besemer, C. (1999):
Mediation. Vermittlung in Konflikten. Stiftung Gewaltfreies Leben. Werkstatt für Gewaltfreie Aktion, Baden. Sechste Auflage.

Blalock, H. (1989):
Power and Conflict. Towards a General Theory. London.

Bond, M. (1988)
Finding Universal Dimensions of Individual Variation in Multicultural Studies of Values: The Rokeach and Chinese Value Surveys. In: Journal of Personality and Social Psychology.1988, Vol 55, No. 6, S. 1009-1015.

Bond (1998), M.
Social Psychology Across Cultures. 2. Edition, Prentice Hall Europe,Hertfordshire.

Boness, C. (2002):
Kritische Situationen in Begegnungen zwischen Tansaniern und Europäern. Eine Felduntersuchung im Secondary School System Tansanias. Peter Lang Verlag, Frankfurt.

Boness, C. & Mayer, C.-H. (2003):
Ostafrikanische Kulturstandards. In. Handbuch interkulturelle Kommunikation und Kooperation. Band 2: Länder, Kulturen und interkulturelle Berufstätigkeit. Herausgegeben von Alexander Thomas, Stefan Kammhuber, Sylvia Schroll-Machl.

Bourdieu, P. (1982):
Die feinen Unterschiede. Kritik der Gesellschaftlichen Urteilskraft.
Frankfurt/M.

Coetzee, P.H. (1998):
Paricularity in Morality and its Reation to Community. In: Coetzee, P.H./
Roux, A.P.J., Philosophy from Africa. A text with readings.International
Thomson Publishing (Southern
Africa), S. 275-291
Johannesburg: Halfway House

Coetzee,P.H./ Roux, A.P.J. (Eds) (1998):
Philosophy from Africa. A text with readings.International Publishing
Southern Africa

Dadder, R. (1987):
Interkulturelle Orientierung: Analyse ausgewählter interkultureller
Orientierungsprogramme. Saarbrücken.

Daily, J. (1991):
The Effects of Anger on Negotiations over Mengers and Aquisitions.
In: Negotiation Journal, 1991, 7(1), S.31-29.

D'Andrade, R. (1985):
Character Terms and Cultural Models.
In: Dougherty, J.W.D. (1985)(Hrsg.): Directions in Cognitive
Anthropology. University of Illinois Press. Urbana and Chicago, S. 321-343.

D'Andrade, R. (1992):
Cognitive Anthropology.
In: Lutz, C.A. & Schwartz, T. & White, G. M: (1992)(Hrsg.): New
Directions in Psychological Anthropology. Cambridge University Press,
S. 47-59.

Devine, P. (1989):
Stereotypes and prejudice. In: Journal of Personality and Social Psychology, 56, 5-18.

Dulabaum, N.L. (1998):
Mediation: Das ABC. Die Kunst, in Konflikten erfolgreich zu vermitteln. 2. Auflage. Beltz Verlag, Weinheim und Basel.

Fisher, G. (1998):
The Mindsets Factor in Ethnic Conflict. A Cross-Cultural Agenda. Intercultural Press, Yarmouth.

Flechsig, K.-H. (1996):
Einführung in die interkulturelle Didaktik. Internes Skript. Göttingen, Juli 1996.

Flechsig, K.-H. (2001):
Beiträge zum Interkulturellen Training. Erstfassung Juni 2001. Interne Arbeitspapiere. Copyright Institut für Interkulturelle Didaktik e.V.

Glasl, F. (1997):
Konfliktmanagement. Ein Handbuch für Führungskräfte, Beraterinnen und Berater. 6. Auflage. Verlag Freies Geistesleben, Stuttgart.

Glasl, F. (2000):
Selbsthilfe in Konflikten. Konzepte, Übungen, Praktische Methoden. 2. Auflage. Verlag Freies Geistesleben, Stuttgart.

Gudykunst, W. B. (Hg.)(1985):
Communication, Culture and Organisational Processes. Sage Publications, California.

Gudykunst, W.B. (1991):
Bridging Differences. Effective intergroup Communication. Sage, Newbury Park.

Gyekeye, K. (1998):
Person and community in African thought. In: Coetzee, P.H./ Roux, A.P.J., Philosophy from Africa. A Text with Readings. International Thomson Publishing (Southern Africa), Johannesburg: Halfway House, S. 317-336

Habermas, J (1981):
Theorie des Kommunikativen Handelns. Band 1 und Band 2. Frankfurt/Main.

Habermas, J. (1984):
Vorstudien und Ergänzungen zur Theorie des kommunikativen Handelns. Frankfurt/Main.

Hall, E. T. (1990):
The Silent Language. Anchor Books, New York.

Haumersen, P., Liebe, F. (1999):
Multikulti-Konflikte konstruktiv. Trainingshandbuch. Mediation in der interkulturellen Arbeit. Verlag an der Ruhr, Mühlheim.

Hofstede, G. (1985):
Culture's Consequences: International Differences in Work-Related Values. Abridged Edition, Beverly Hills CA: Sage Publications, London.

Hofstede, G. (1993):
Interkulturelle Zusammenarbeit: Kulturen Organisationen-Management. Gabler, Wiesbaden.

Hofstede, G. (1997):
Lokales Denken, Globales Handeln. Kulturen, Zusammenarbeit und Management. Beck-Wirtschaftsberater im DTV-Taschenbuchverlag.

Honneth, A. (1994):
Kampf um Anerkennung. Zur moralischen Grammatik sozialer Konflikte. Frankfurt/M.

Hoopes, D. & Ventura, P. (Hrsg.)(1979):
Intercultural Sourcebook. Cross-Cultural Trainings Methodologies. Intercultural N, LaGrange Park.

Johnson, F. (1978)(Ed.):
A Standard Swahili-English Dictionary. Oxford University Press, Nairobi 1939. This Edition, 1978.

Kim, U. et al. (1994):
Individualism and Collectivism. Theory, Method and Applications. Cross-cultural Researchand Methodology Series, Vol. 18.Sage Publications, Thousand Oaks, London.

Kluckhohn, F.R. & Stroedbeck, F. L.(1961)
Variations in Value Orientations. IL: Row and Peterson, Evanston.

Kohls, L. R. & Knight, J. M. (1994):
Developing Intercultural Awareness. A Cross-Cultural Training Handbook. Second Edition. Intercultural Press.

Kolb, D. A. (1984):
Experimental Learning. Prentice Hall, New York.

Krewer, B. (1994):
Interkulturelle Trainingsprogramme - Bestandsaufnahme und Perspektiven.
In: Nouveaux Cahiers d' Allemend 1994, S. 139ff.

Kroeber, A. & Kluckhohn, C. (1952):
Culture. A Critical Review of Concepts and Definitions. Cambridge, Mass.

Lange, C. (1994):
Interkulturelle Orientierung am Beispiel der Trainingsmethode "Cultural Assimilator":
In: Beiträge zur Interkulturellen Didaktik, Band 3. Göttingen.

Lederach, J.P. (1988):
„Of Nets, Nails and Problems: A Folk Vision of Conflict in Central America".
Ph.D. diss., University of Colorado.

Lederach, J.P. (1989):
Director's Circle. In: Conciliation Quarterly, 8:3, Summer 1998, S. 12-14.

Lederach, J.P. (1995):
Preparing for Peace: Conflict Transformation Across Cultures. Syracuse University Press, New York.

Lederach, J.P. (1996):
Preparing for Peace. Conflict Transformation Across Cultures. Paperback Edition. Syracuse University Press, New York.

Liebe, F. (1996):
Interkulturelle Mediation - eine schwierige Vermittlung. Eine empirische Annäherung zur Bedeutung von kulturellen Unterschieden. Berghof Forschungszentrum für konstruktive Konfliktbearbeitung. Berghof Report Nr. 2, Mai 1996, Berlin.

Luhmann, N. (1987):
Soziale Systeme. Grundriß einer Allgemeinen Theorie. Frankfurt/M.

Lutz, C.A. (1988):
Unnatural Emotions. Everyday Sentiments on a Micronesian Atoll & their Challenge to Western Theory. The University Chicago Press, LTD, London.

Lyotard, J.-F. (1987):
Der Widerstreit. München

Matsumoto, D. et al (1997):
Context Specific Measurement of Individualism - Collectivism on the individual level.
In: Journal of Cross-Cultural Psychology, Nov. 1997, Thousand Oaks.

Mayer, C.-H.(2001):
Werteorientierungen an Sekundarschulen in Tanzania vor dem Hintergrund interkulturelle und inner-afrikanischer Wertediskussionen. Ibidem-Verlag, Stuttgart.

Mayer, C.-H., Boness, C., Thomas, A. (2003):
Beruflich in Kenia und Tansania. Trainingsprogramm für Manager, Fach- & Führungskräfte. Vanderhoeck & Ruprecht, Göttingen.

Mayer, C.-H., Boness, C., Thomas, A. (2004):
Beruflich in Südafrika. Trainingsprogramm für Manager, Fach- & Führungskräfte. Vanderhoeck & Ruprecht, Göttingen.

Mayer, C.-H. (2005):
Interkulturelle Mediation im Spannungsfeld westlicher und afrikanischer Perspektiven. In: Busch, D. (Ed.) (2005): Interkulturelle Mediation. Peter Lang Verlag. In Publishing Process.

Mbiti, J. S. (1974)
Afrikanische Religion und Weltanschauung. De Gruyter, Berlin.

Mead, G.-H. (1968):
Geist, Identität und Gesellschaft. Suhrkamp Verlag, Frankurt a. M.

Myers. S: & Filner, B . and IDI (1994):
Mediation across Cultures. A Handbook about Conflict and Culture. San Diego Mediation Centre, Amherst Educational Publishing, San Diego.

Prätorius, R. (1985):
Konflikttheorie. In: Nohlen, D. & Schulze, R.-O. (Hrsg.) (1985): Politikwissenschaft. Theorien, Methoden, Begriffe. München.

Quinn, N. (1982).
"Commitment" in American Marriage: A Cultural Analysis. In: American Ethnologist, 9, S. 775-798.

Ricci, I. (1980):
Mom's House, Dad's House. Collier Books, New York.

Röttger-Rössler, B. (1997):
Die Wortlosigkeit des Ethnologen: zum Problem der Übersetzung zwischen den Kulturen am Beispiel Indonesischer Gefühlstermini. In: Bachmann-Medick, D. (Hrsg.) Übersetzung als Repräsentation fremder Kulturen. Sonderdruck. Erich Schmidt Verlag, S. 199-213.

Ripke, L. (1999):
Charakteristika eines guten Abschlussvertrages. Perspektiven und Prinzipien der Mediation. In: KonSens - Zeitschrift für Mediation, 2,6, 1999, S. 341-343.

Ropers, N. (1995):
Friedliche Einmischung. Strukturen, Prozesse und Strategien zur konstruktiven Bearbeitung ethnopolitischer Konflikte. Berghof Report Nr. 1.Berghof Forschungszentrum für konstruktive Konfliktbearbeitung, Berlin.

Rosaldo, M.Z. (1984):
Toward an Anthropology of Self and Feeling. In: Shweder, R.A. & Levine R.A. (1984): Culture Theory. Essays on Mind, Self, and Emotion. Cambridge University Press, Cambridge, S. 137-158.

Rosenberg, D.V. (1990):
Language in the Discourse of Emotions. In: Lutz, C.A. & Abu-Lughod, L. (1990)(Hrsg.): Language and the Politics of Emotion. Cambridge University Press, Cambridge, S. 162-185.

Rosenberg, M. (2001):
Gewaltfreie Kommunikation. Junfermann Verlag, Paderborn.

Schwartz, S. (1994):
Are there Universal Aspects in the Structure and Content of Human Values?
In: Mayton, Lodges et al (1994): Human Values and Social Sciences. Journal of Social Issues, Vol 50, No. 4, Winter 1994, S. 19-45.

Shweder, R.A: (1991):
Thinking through Cultures. Expeditions in Cultural Psychology. Harvard University Press, Cambridge.

Simmel, G. (1992):
Der Streit. In: Soziologie. Untersuchung über die Formen der Vergesellschaftung. Gesamtausgabe Band 2. Frankfurt/M.

Taasisi (1981)
Taasisi ya Uchunguzi wa Kiswahili. Kamusi ya Kiswahili sanifu. Oxford University Press, Nairobi

Teffo, L. J. /Roux, A. P. J. (1998):
Metaphysical Thinking in Africa. In: Coettzee, P.H./ Roux, A.P.J. (1998): Philosophy from Africa. A Text with Readings. International Thomson Publishing., Johannesburg, S. 134-148.

Teunissen, E., Walsfisz, B. (1993):
Intercultural Cooperation between Germans and Tansanians. ITIM/ GTZ. Frankfurt Eschborn

Ting-Toomey, S. (1985):
Towards a Theory of Conflict and Culture. In: Gudykunst, S. & Ting-Toomey, S. (1985): Communication, Culture and Organisational Processes. Newbury Park, CA: Sage, S. 71-86.

Ting-Toomey, S. & Oetzel, J. G. (2001)
Managing Intercultural Conflict Effektively. Sage Publications. Thousand Oaks.

Thomas, A. & Schenk, E. (2001):
Beruflich in China.Trainingsprogramm für Manager, Fach- und Führungskräfte.
V & R, Göttingen.

Triandis, H. C. (1986):
Approaches to Cross- Cultural Orientation and the Role of Culture Assimilator Training. In: Paige, R.M. (ed), Cross- Cultural Orientation; New Conceptualizations and Applications. (S.193-222), Boston.

Triandis, H.C. (1994):
Culture and Social Behavior.in: McGraw-Hill series in social psychology. Illinois

Triandis, H. C. (1995):
Individualism & Collectivism. Westview Press, Boulder, San Francisco, Oxford.

Watzlawik, P., Weakland, J. und Fisch, R. (1978):
Change. W.W. Norton, New York.

Watzlawik, P., Beavin, J.H., Jackson, D.D. (1985):
Menschliche Kommunikation. 7. Auflage, Bern.

Watzlawick, P. (Hrsg.)(2001):
Die erfundene Wirklichkeit. Wie wissen wir, was wir zu wissen glauben? Beiträge zum Konstruktivismus. 13. Auflage. Piper Verlag, Gmbh München.

Watzlawick, P. (2001a):
Selbsterfüllende Prophezeiungen. In: Watzlawick, P. (Hrsg.)(2001): Die erfundene Wirklichkeit. Wie wir wissen, was wir zu wissen glauben? Beiträge zum Konstruktivismus. 13. Auflage. Piper Verlag, Gmbh München. S.91-110.

Weede, E. (1986):
Konfliktforschung. Leske und Budrich, Opladen

Weiß, A. (2001):
Macht und Differenz. Ein erweitertes Modell der Konfliktpotentiale in interkulturellen Auseinandersetzungen. Berghof Report Nr. 7: Berghof Forschungszentrum für konstruktive Konfliktbearbeitung, Berlin.

***ibidem*-**Verlag
Melchiorstr. 15
D-70439 Stuttgart

info@ibidem-verlag.de

www.ibidem-verlag.de
www.edition-noema.de
www.autorenbetreuung.de

www.ingramcontent.com/pod-product-compliance
Lightning Source LLC
Chambersburg PA
CBHW051643230426
43669CB00013B/2418